FREDERIC BLOCK

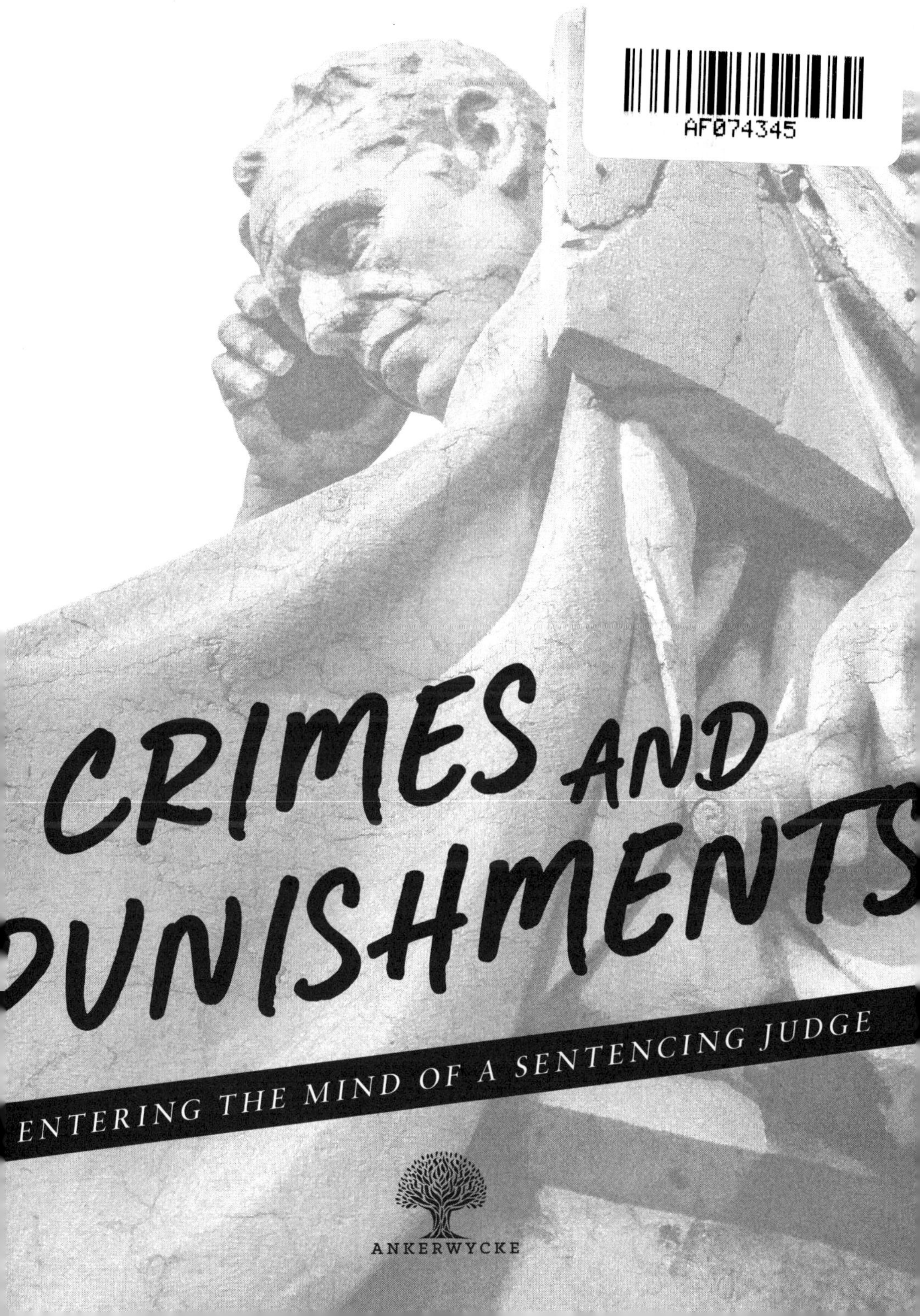

CRIMES AND PUNISHMENTS

ENTERING THE MIND OF A SENTENCING JUDGE

ANKERWYCKE

Cover design by Elmarie Jara/ABA Design.
Interior design by Betsy Kulak/ABA Design.

The materials contained herein represent the opinions of the authors and/or the editors, and should not be construed to be the views or opinions of the law firms or companies with whom such persons are in partnership with, associated with, or employed by, nor of the American Bar Association unless adopted pursuant to the bylaws of the Association.

Nothing contained in this book is to be considered as the rendering of legal advice for specific cases, and readers are responsible for obtaining such advice from their own legal counsel. This book is intended for educational and informational purposes only.

© 2019 Frederic Block. All rights reserved.

No part of this publication may be reproduced, stored in a retrieval system, or transmitted in any form or by any means, electronic, mechanical, photocopying, recording, or otherwise, without the prior written permission of the publisher. For permission contact the ABA Copyrights & Contracts Department, copyright@americanbar.org, or complete the online form at http://www.americanbar.org/utility/reprint.html.

Printed in the United States of America.

23 22 21 20 19   5 4 3 2 1

ISBN: 978-1-64105-381-5

Discounts are available for books ordered in bulk. Special consideration is given to state bars, CLE programs, and other bar-related organizations. Inquire at Book Publishing, ABA Publishing, American Bar Association, 321 N. Clark Street, Chicago, Illinois 60654-7598.

www.ShopABA.org

*For my new baby granddaughter Janice,
who I hope will find my book of value when she grows up.*

Other Works by This Author

Race to Judgment (2017)

Disrobed: An Inside Look at the Life and Work of a Federal Trial Judge (2012)

Coauthor of the musical *Professionally Speaking* (book, music, and lyrics) (1985)

Contents

Foreword — vii
Introduction — xiii

1. Uncharged Criminal Conduct
   David Kent Fitch — 1
2. Acquitted Criminal Conduct
   Anthony Praddy and the Raleigh Place Crew — 19
3. Victim Impact Testimony
   The Carreto Family — 65
4. Mandatory Minimums
   John Doe — 95
5. The Mafia
   Peter Gotti and the Gambinos — 107
6. Public Officials
   Pedro Espada Jr. — 135
7. Collateral Consequences
   Chevelle Nesbeth — 163

Coda — 187
Acknowledgments — 190
About the Author — 191

Foreword

The government has no power greater than to take away a person's freedom or even life. We trust our judges to balance justice and mercy to arrive at an appropriate sentence when a person has been convicted of a crime. Yet to a large extent, how a judge goes about this process is invisible to the lawyers in a case, the public, and even to the criminal defendant being sentenced. To be sure, judges often give reasons for their sentences, such as explaining when their sentence is dictated by a statute requiring a mandatory minimum sentence or how the punishment fits under the sentencing guidelines. But the human dimension of this—how a judge actually balances justice and mercy, what a judge feels in putting a person in prison for a long time or condemning a person to death—is rarely publicly explored.

Judge Frederic Block, a long-time federal district court judge, has written a magnificent book which describes the experience of a human being punishing other human beings. Judge Block does this by telling the stories of some of the cases that he has handled since coming on the bench in 1994. Each of the cases is compelling and Judge Block is a great storyteller. Each evokes important issues concerning our criminal justice system. Judge Block is candid in sharing his thinking and his feelings as he approached imposing punishments in these instances. He is remarkably self-reflective, often describing his concerns that his religion or the unfounded accusations against him or his recent reading might be unduly influencing the sentences he is imposing. Along the way, he tells us a lot about the workings of the federal courts and also about his life.

What comes across most clearly is how Judge Block is trying mightily to follow the law, even when it leads to results he feels are unjust, but also to use his discretion to do what he feels is right: imposing significant penalties when that seems appropriate, but also acting with compassion when that seems warranted. This is a book that can be enjoyed simply for its stories and its humanity. It is about the crimes people commit and what a judge considers in punishing them. It therefore is a book that deserves a wide audience. It is beautifully written and accessible to lawyers and non-lawyers alike.

But there also is an underlying dimension to the book that should be part of a larger conversation about the problems with our current sentencing system. I can identify several important issues that emerge from reading Judge Block's book.

First, there is the problem of draconian punishments and the point at which they become cruel and unusual in violation of the Eighth Amendment. In fact, Judge Block expressly poses the question of when sentences are so disproportionate to the crime as to violate the Eighth Amendment. The first case I ever argued in the Supreme Court was *Lockyer v. Andrade*, where my client received a sentence of fifty years to life, with no possibility of parole for fifty years, for stealing $153 worth of videotapes from K-Mart stores in San Bernardino, California. He received this sentence even though he had never committed a violent crime and even though no one in the history of the United States had received a life sentence for shoplifting until California's "three strikes law."

The United States Court of Appeals for the Ninth Circuit ruled that the sentence was unconstitutional cruel and unusual punishment, but the Supreme Court reversed in a 5–4 decision. In *Lockyer v. Andrade* and a companion case, *Ewing v. California*, the Court made clear that the government has enormous discretion in imposing punishments, even very lengthy sentences for minor crimes.

In the story of "John Doe," Judge Block tells of imposing a mandatory minimum sentence of fifteen years in a case where that seems clearly excessive. As a conscientious judge following the law, Judge Block imposed this punishment even though he thought it was excessive under the circumstances. It made me think about being a judge when the law requires an unjust, though constitutional result. Laws like "mandatory minimums" and "three strikes" often require this of our judges. The "tough on crime" mentality of the last half century has led to legislatures, and sometimes voters, sometimes creating punishments that are far too harsh for the crimes involved. No politician wants to seem soft on crime. Judge Block tells what it is like to be a judge having to apply these laws.

Second, laws like these—such as mandatory minimums and three strikes—have meant a significant shift of power in sentencing from judges to prosecutors. In the John Doe case, it was the prosecutor's choice to charge and try the case under a statute that required a mandatory minimum penalty that tied Judge Block's hands. In *Lockyer v. Andrade*, the prosecutor could have charged Leandro Andrade with one misdemeanor count of petty theft, with a maximum sentence of six months in jail; or two counts of petty theft, with a maximum sentence of one year in jail; or one count of the felony of "petty theft with a prior," with a maximum sentence of three years in prison; or two counts of petty theft with a prior, with a maximum sentence of three years, eight months in prison; or one count under the three strikes law, with a maximum sentence of twenty-five years to life in prison; or two counts under the three strikes law, with a maximum sentence of fifty years in prison. The charging decision was left entirely to the prosecutor and he choose the maximum possible. The judge was helpless to prevent this and the jury that convicted had no idea as to the consequences of their verdicts.

I am troubled by the great shift in the power to determine sentences from judges to prosecutors. This change in the law has not received nearly enough attention. Prosecutors are partisans in our criminal justice system. No matter how much it is said that a prosecutor's role is to secure justice, they see sentencing from their own perspective. It is far better to have sentencing decisions in the hands of judges, but that is very much lessened when the prosecutor's charging decisions make all the difference in terms of the punishment imposed.

Third, Judge Block describes the enormously disturbing reality that defendants can be sentenced for crimes for which they are not convicted and even for crimes for which they were acquitted. This is reflected in the first two chapters of Judge Block's book, one involving a case that he heard while sitting by designation in the United States Court of Appeals for the Ninth Circuit and the other he handled as a district court judge.

The law is clear that a judge in sentencing may impose punishments for crimes for which the defendant was acquitted. In *United States v. Watts* (1997), the Supreme Court held that a jury's verdict of acquittal does not prevent a sentencing court from considering a defendant's conduct underlying the acquitted charge, so long as that conduct has been proved by a preponderance of the evidence. The rationale is that a conclusion of guilt requires proof beyond a reasonable doubt, but a sentencing factor need be proven only by preponderance of the evidence.

I always have felt that it unjust for a person to be punished for a crime for which he or she has been acquitted. Imagine a defendant is charged with twelve counts, eleven for very serious offenses and one for something minor. If the defendant is acquitted on the eleven serious counts, he or she can still be punished for them if convicted of the minor crime.

This is exactly what happened in the cases that Judge Block describes. The law allows it, but I hope the Supreme Court will reverse its earlier opinion and find that it is unconstitutional to punish someone for a crime for which he or she has been acquitted.

Fourth, throughout the book, Judge Block refers to the sentencing guidelines. These were adopted over thirty years ago to create more uniformity in sentencing. As Judge Block explains, they create a system that requires that a judge consider a number of prescribed factors and it yields a range for the permissible sentence. The U.S. Supreme Court in *United States v. Booker* (2005) held the guidelines are advisory, not mandatory. Judges, though, must still justify departures from what the guidelines prescribe.

As I read Judge Block referring repeatedly to the "guidelines range," I was interested in knowing more about his thinking about the sentencing guidelines. Many, including judges I have spoken to, believe that they are too harsh. Some think they went too far in substituting uniformity for individualized sentencing. But others think that *Booker*'s making the guidelines advisory has helped to cure this problem. After more than thirty years' experience with the guidelines, and more than a decade since *Booker*, it is time for a careful examination of how they function and whether they are desirable.

Finally, Judge Block's book forces us to continue to think carefully about the role of race in the criminal justice system. This especially comes up in the last chapter about Chevelle Nesbeth, a young woman who was convicted of attempting to smuggle cocaine in the United States.

Judge Block describes focusing on the collateral consequences of her conviction, all of the ways in which Nesbeth would be harmed by a criminal conviction. A felony conviction often is a lifetime disqualification from occupational licenses; in some places, it prevents people from being able to vote. In telling the story of Nesbeth's sentencing, Judge Block examined whether these consequences should be taken into account in deciding her punishment. In one of the more powerful passages, Judge Block describes having just read Michelle Alexander's book, *The New Jim Crow*. Professor Alexander powerfully details the collateral consequences of criminal convictions, especially in terms of their effects on defendants of color.

This caused Judge Block to write a forty-two-page opinion and to impose a sentence substantially lower than the sentence guidelines range. It also caused Judge Block to instruct the probation department to include a collateral consequences section in all future presentence reports. Hopefully, other judges will copy this practice. It should be part of a larger consideration of race in the criminal justice system.

These, of course, are just some of the issues and some of the stories in this wonderful book. Most of all, in reading the book I came away with the sense that regardless of whether I was a prosecutor or a defense lawyer, I would want Judge Block to be hearing my cases. I hope it never happens, but if I or someone I love committed a crime, I would want Judge Block to decide the sentence. I came away from the book with a strong sense that Judge Block does all that a human being possibly can to be conscientious, thoughtful, and fair in imposing punishment. And that is all, as lawyers and as citizens, we can expect of our judges. I am so glad that he wrote this book and gave us the chance to understand his thinking in making the profoundly important decisions about how to punish people for their crimes.

—**Erwin Chemerinsky**
Dean and Jesse H. Choper Distinguished Professor of Law,
University of California, Berkeley School of Law

Introduction

He had one leg and a crutch for the missing one. Darryl Fulton had just been convicted for a string of bank robberies, and as he wobbled toward me, I started to hyperventilate. I was about to sentence someone to jail for the first time as a newly minted federal district judge.

That was twenty-four years ago. Since then I have probably put more than a thousand people in jail. It is the toughest part of the job.

For this book, I have picked out a cross-section of several different crimes for which I had to sentence a convicted criminal. I first write about their crimes. For example, I tell the stories of the trials of Peter Gotti (who succeeded his brother John as head of the Gambino crime family) and Pedro Espada Jr. (the former leader of the New York Senate). I then take the reader through the sentencing proceedings. I recount what the defendants said, what the lawyers said, what the victims said, and what I said. And I share with you my private thoughts and doubts as to whether I imposed the right sentence: Should I have sentenced Gotti to more than nine years? Was five years the right number for Espada? And each chapter represents a different sentencing category. For example, it will undoubtedly come as a surprise that a federal judge can consider *uncharged* and even *acquitted* conduct in rendering the sentence.

There is no uniformity in the sentences judges hand out. Regardless of all sorts of sentencing guidelines and multiple efforts throughout the years to try to avoid sentencing disparities among similarly situated criminals, every criminal defense lawyer will tell you that who the judge is still makes all the difference in the world.

Justice Sotomayor's book *My Beloved World* provides a better understanding of how her compelling beginnings shape her thinking as she wades through the challenging issues she must decide as the first Hispanic Supreme Court justice. And learning of Chief Justice Roberts's far different upbringing allows us to appreciate how his thoughts might be different from his colleague's. It is not a matter of right or wrong. They are both skilled, dedicated jurists who care passionately about doing the right thing. And we would not want it to be any different. We do not want all the justices to be of one mind-set. Diversity of attitudes, opinions, and thoughts make for a more robust court.

When it comes to sentencing, however, we may not want such diversity. Conceptually, criminals doing the same crime should be doing the same time. But that is not how it works in the real world, any more than in the Supreme Court. As we will see, our sentencing laws give judges an enormous amount of discretion, and judges coming from different parts of the country, with different sociocultural backgrounds, will rarely see eye-to-eye. Our life stories are all different, and they shape our thought processes. No one makes a decision in a vacuum. We are the products of our environments, our families, our life experiences.

And the age of the judge and the number of years on the bench usually make a huge difference. There is a tendency for the new judge to be more cautious and less likely to stray from the straight and narrow. The sentences imposed during the staging-in phase of the judge's career will probably be greater than the sentences imposed under similar circumstances when the judge has a few years under his or her belt.

Conversely, since federal judges are appointed by the president for life, be wary of the very old judge whose perspective may be entirely different. I recall when I first got on the bench meeting the venerable Judge Bartels, who at the tender age of ninety-six was still sitting after four decades. He never remembered my name and would call me Sonny. We all loved him. He died just short of his hundredth birthday. But when he was in his nineties, he was still putting people in jail. The story goes that on one occasion, shortly after the judge had turned ninety, a lawyer was pleading that if he gave his client a twenty-year sentence, it would be tantamount to life since he was very old. The good judge asked how old he was. The lawyer said "seventy." Judge Bartels snapped back: "Seems like a pretty young man to me." He gave him the twenty years.

Thus, the sentences that I write about in this book will not necessarily have been the same sentences that my judicial colleagues may have imposed, nor the same sentences that you would have imposed. Nonetheless, I think there is value in confessing to what goes on in at least one judge's mind to provide a window into the real world of sentencing.

It will be easy to do this for things I am consciously aware of. For example, I know that I am troubled and upset whenever I must sentence a Hasidic Jew. I am Jewish and feel ashamed that a fellow Jew— let alone an extremely observant one—has committed a crime. I have disciplined myself, however, by engaging in an internal dialogue to make sure that my angst will not become an unwarranted sentencing factor and that I will not impose a higher sentence than one that a non-Jewish colleague might render. If I had any doubts in a particular situation, I would recuse myself—although that has yet to happen.

But I have no control over the subconscious thoughts that may unwittingly be at play. I can only trust that my upbringing and life experiences have given me a decent judicial compass. What enters my mind when I decide whether someone should be put in jail—and for how long—is therefore the product of both the subconscious and the conscious.

In this book, I share thoughts that entered my mind during the course of the trials. I also recount parts of my life experiences that could have had some impact on my subconscious and may have affected the sentences that I handed out. This is detailed in the wide array of fascinating chapters that follow.

I wrote a good chunk of this book a few years ago but put it on the shelf until I was asked by Law360 to review *Tough Cases* (New Press 2018), a terrific compilation of the inner thoughts that many of our country's fine judges share with the public about the times when they were faced with making difficult decisions. I was struck by their candor in disclosing their "insights into the private thoughts that contribute to a judge's decision." After all, as I also wrote: "What goes on in a judge's mind is the fuel that ignites her or his judgment. It is the human side of our awesome calling, yet we invariably choose not to disclose our judgments' mental underpinnings."

Tough Cases gave me the courage to finish this book, since I think that the public is entitled to know what sentencing is all about and what a judge's inner thoughts are when discharging this awesome aspect of his or her judicial responsibilities.

Crimes and Punishments is also intended to stimulate debate. Should a sentencing judge be allowed to consider uncharged, let alone acquitted conduct? How much weight should victim impact testimony have? How much consideration should be given to the status of a defendant as a public official? Are the RICO laws fair? Should Congress have unfettered discretion to take sentencing away from the judge by establishing mandatory minimum sentences whenever it wishes to do so? Has Congress effectively rendered the sentencing judge a mere functionary in those areas where it has chosen to act? Has Congress gone overboard in setting high mandatory minimums in child pornography cases? How does the prosecutor's charging decision impact sentencing? Is it time for needed reform in respect to the thousands of state and federal statutes establishing significant collateral consequences that ex-felons face? To what extent should these collateral consequences be sentencing factors?

The book raises these issues in what is intended to be reader-friendly dramatic chapters. I hope you will enjoy them.

1

Uncharged Criminal Conduct

David Kent Fitch

The Crime

I have chosen to lead off with the Fitch case because it is a stark example of the extraordinary power of the sentencing judge—and, by contrast, the relatively minor role of the jury—and goes to the heart of necessarily understanding what sentencing is really all about.

David Kent Fitch had been indicted and convicted after a jury trial for several garden-variety, low-level crimes related to the fraudulent use of the credit card and bank account of his wife, who had mysteriously disappeared. The typical sentence for these types of crimes is a couple of years. Nevada federal district judge James Mahan sentenced Fitch to 262 months—just shy of twenty-two years—because he decided that Fitch must have killed his wife. The judge did this even though Fitch was neither convicted—nor even indicted and tried—for murdering her. And for all we know, she might even be alive.

The *Fitch* case is the only one in this book where I was not the sentencing judge. I was acting as a designated circuit court appellate judge for the Ninth Circuit Court of Appeals. The country is divided into twelve federal circuits. The circuit courts' function is to review the decisions of the federal district courts. The Ninth Circuit is the largest circuit. It handles appeals from the district courts of California and eight other western states, including Nevada. Circuit courts sit in three-judge panels. One of the judges can be a district court judge; the other two must be circuit judges.

Because of the heavy case load of the Ninth Circuit, district court judges are frequently asked to help out. They need not come from a state within the circuit. Even though I am a district court judge from Brooklyn, I have been invited many times to sit as a designated Ninth Circuit Court of Appeals judge, and I had to decide—together with the two circuit court appellate judges—whether the law permitted Judge Mahan to sentence Fitch for a crime he was never charged with committing, let alone one for murder.

In 1997 and 1998, David Fitch spent considerable time in Bogotá, Colombia, where he became romantically involved with Patricia Molano Gutierrez, a Colombian citizen. Patricia moved to England in early 1998, and in mid-1998 Fitch traveled to England to visit her.

While in England, Fitch met Maria Bozi. Romanian by birth, Maria was a naturalized citizen of the United Kingdom and had lived and worked in England since 1991. Although still romantically involved with Patricia, Fitch married Maria in England on April 23, 1999.

A few weeks after their wedding, Fitch went to the United States while Maria remained in England and prepared to leave. She sublet her apartment and shipped, sold, or stored her personal property. She also opened a U.S. bank account in her name only, at Citibank. She transferred $120,000 into the account in July 1999.

Maria stayed with a former boyfriend, Michael Novin, for a few weeks before she left England. She used Novin's mailing address for her bank and credit card statements. At the end of July, Novin drove Maria to the airport, where she took a flight to Nevada to meet her new husband.

Soon after arriving in Nevada, Maria purchased a 1994 Ford Thunderbird. She registered the car in her name only. She also purchased a $14,000 mobile home and leased space for it at the Lakeshore Trailer Village in the Lake Mead National Recreation Area. Maria was the sole tenant on the lease and listed herself as the sole owner of the mobile home. She and her husband moved into the mobile home at the end of August 1999.

Maria would regularly telephone her mother in Romania and Novin in England, but the calls stopped a few days after she and David moved into the mobile home. Novin last spoke to Maria on September 4, when she told him that she and her husband were going on a "mini trip" for a week or two and that she would call him when she returned. Maria did not tell Novin where she and David were going.

Between September 7 and 17, 1999, David withdrew a total of $8,000 from Maria's Citibank account. On one occasion, he made the withdrawal while wearing a hat, sunglasses, and a fake mustache. On September 10, he purchased an $8,000 cashier's check payable to Patricia Molano.

The next day, a Citibank representative called Novin trying to reach Maria regarding, in Novin's words, "some checks and some urgent matter." Novin gave the caller Maria's phone number in the United States.

On September 13, David Fitch deposited a $40,000 check drawn on Maria's Citibank account into his own account. Four days later, Citibank froze Maria's account.

On September 18, Novin attempted to contact Maria to discuss Citibank's phone call and left a message on her answering machine. David returned Novin's call "half an hour later" and told Novin that Maria had "gone ahead to Vancouver because she had found a job there." At roughly the same time, David told Grace Silvers, a neighbor, that Maria "went back to England."

Concerned that he had not heard from Maria in several days, Novin contacted the U.S. Park Service. Prompted by Novin's phone call, park ranger Gary Sebade visited David Fitch on September 29. Fitch told Sebade that Maria had returned to Romania. Earlier that same day, Fitch—calling himself "Mario Bozi"—had used Maria's health insurance card and account number to schedule hernia surgery for October 5.

On October 1, park rangers saw Fitch loading his truck at the trailer park. They followed him to a dumpster, where they saw him discard several items. Searching the dumpster, the rangers found a receipt, dated July 7, 1999, reflecting the purchase of chloroform by a "Dr. David."

Now suspecting foul play, the rangers sealed Maria's mobile home with police tape. Fitch did not return to the trailer park, but instead checked into a motel in Las Vegas. On October 9, Maria's Thunderbird was stolen and the police-tape barrier was broken.

At some point in October, Fitch attempted to sell Lorinda Brodoski "a women's clothing and shoes and just personal items for a woman [her] size." Brodoski testified at trial that Fitch had told her "he was selling these things because his wife left him." Later that month, Fitch attempted to use Maria's credit card to purchase $5,000 in synthetic emeralds over the Internet; the card was declined.

While in Las Vegas, Fitch met a man named David Lee Krause. Fitch convinced Krause to give him his personal information, which Fitch then used to obtain duplicates of Krause's Social Security card and birth certificate. Using those documents, Fitch obtained a Utah's driver's license and U.S. passport; both bore Fitch's photograph but Krause's name.

Fitch used the Krause passport to travel to London on November 25. There, he married Patricia Molano using his assumed identity.

Fitch reentered the United States on February 7, 2000, again using the Krause passport. The following day, officers with the Henderson (Nevada) Police Department stopped Fitch for speeding. He was driving the 1994 Thunderbird and presented the Krause driver's license as identification. A routine license plate search revealed the connection to Maria, prompting the officers to contact the FBI. The FBI asked them to detain Fitch until federal agents could get to the scene. Since the license plate search had also revealed outstanding warrants against Fitch, the officers placed him under arrest.

Fitch's arrest triggered a full FBI investigation. Between February 8 and 25, 2000, agents seized from Fitch, inter alia, a shotgun, three rifles, a revolver, a box of shotgun shells, numerous books, a passport in the name of Maria Bozi, and a "briefcase with miscellaneous documents" in her name. They also recovered the Krause birth certificate, passport, and driver's license.

In addition, the FBI sought information from potential witnesses living in Romania and the United Kingdom through Mutual Legal Assistance Treaty (MLAT) requests. As a result of those MLAT requests, the FBI received witness statements from Michael Novin, Patricia Molano, and others. None of the potential witnesses had any knowledge of Maria's whereabouts.

In March 2003, the FBI interviewed Fitch's father. He stated that his son had married a woman in England but could not recall her name. When asked about Maria Bozi, he stated that he had "no knowledge" of her.

To date, Maria's whereabouts remain unknown.

The Punishment

How could Judge Mahan have sentenced Fitch to jail for just about a quarter century for killing his wife if he was never charged with murdering her and the jury only convicted him for the relatively minor crimes stemming from the fraudulent use of Maria Bozi's credit card and bank account? You have probably scratched your head and asked, "What is going on here?" To unravel this seeming paradox, we need to understand key aspects of the history of sentencing in our country and the fundamental differences between the role of the jury and the role of the sentencing judge. But it is not my purpose to write extensively on the evolution of sentencing laws and theories of penology that have been bandied about and implemented at various times throughout the years since the birth of our country. There are many scholarly books that do this. Here I try to simply focus on the real world of sentencing that I live with every day.

Congress has the power to fix the sentence for a federal crime. Early on, it chose to abandon fixed-sentence rigidity, except for mandatory life sentences for certain murder-related crimes, and put in place a system of ranges within which the sentencing judge could determine the precise punishment. But the outer ranges were invariably very high. And for most crimes there were either no or relatively low mandatory minimums. Thus, the judge could fix the sentence within any point in this huge range. As the Supreme Court has recognized: "Congress delegated almost unfettered discretion to the sentencing judge to determine what the sentence should be within the customarily wide range so selected." This broad discretion was further enhanced by the power of the judge to grant probation and to even suspend the sentence. Moreover, there was virtually no appellate review. As long as the judge did not exceed the broad maximums fixed by Congress or did not fail to adhere to a mandatory minimum, the sentence could not be reversed.

Federal parole boards decided whether the prisoner should be returned to the general population before the expiration of the sentence, but this could not happen until the criminal had served a substantial period of time. Parole board members presumably were skilled to assess when, if at all, a prisoner was rehabilitated. The membership of each parole board for each federal institution, when parole was first implemented for federal prisoners at the turn of the twentieth century, consisted of the warden and physician of the institution and the superintendent of prisons of the Department of Justice.

Things were—and are—different on the state levels. There is great variety among the states. Some have fixed determinative sentencing, where each crime carries a specific sentence. Some have indeterminate sentencing systems. Some have a mixture of both based upon the particular crime. But even where there are indeterminate sentencing regimes, the ranges fixed by the states' legislatures significantly cabin in the judge's discretion. For example, to this day, bank fraud in New York State carries a range of one to four years, but on the federal level, it is zero to thirty years.

The unfettered sentencing discretion that federal judges had did not sit well with a rising tide of public sentiment that took root in the later part of the twentieth century, calling for some semblance of uniformity and consistency in federal sentencing. As Judge Marvin E. Frankel, often referred to as the "father of [federal] sentencing reform," wrote: "[T]he almost wholly unchecked and sweeping powers we give to [federal] judges in the fashioning of sentences are terrifying and intolerable for a society that professes devotion to the rule of law."

Congress responded. In 1984 it passed the Sentencing Reform Act, creating the United States Sentencing Commission. Its purpose was to prepare sentencing guidelines—subject to Congress's approval—in an effort to create sentencing uniformity so that similarly situated defendants throughout the country would be given similar sentences. The new sentencing regime abolished parole and created a determinate sentencing system. Now, if you did the crime, you truly had to do the time, except you could get 15 percent off if you behaved yourself while in jail.

Under this new regime, each crime created by Congress carried a base level number of points. For example, the most serious crime—premeditated murder—carried 43 points. The least serious crime got 4 points. To this base level you might have to add additional points. Thus, if the defendant was a leader or organizer in the criminal activity, he might qualify for up to 3 more points. There were a host of other possibilities for stacking up points. And there were some possibilities for lowering them; for example, if the defendant had pleaded guilty—sparing the government of a trial—he could get 2 or 3 points deducted for acceptance of responsibility.

Once you arrived at the total points associated with the crime, you would then have to determine what criminal history category the defendant fell into. If the defendant had no prior criminal brushes with the law, he would be in category I. If he had prior convictions, he would get criminal history points. A serious prior felony would carry 3 points; a less serious crime might only require 1 point. The criminal history categories ranged from I through VI—correlated to the total number of points. For example, if the defendant had more than 12 points, he would get the top prize—category VI, which is reflective of a really bad apple.

After you calculated the correct number of points associated with the crime and the appropriate criminal history category, a grid would tell you what the range of punishment should be. For example, 17 points and a criminal history of III would carry a sentencing range of thirty to thirty-seven months; 43 points—regardless of the criminal history category—would be life. The judge could sentence the defendant to any point within the range. In doing so, although the seriousness of the crime had to be considered, the judge could also take into account the defendant's individual characteristics. Thus, the judge was entitled to consider the defendant's age, education, physical or mental problems, military service, prior good deeds, employment history, family or community ties, lack of youthful guidance, and socioeconomic status.

But those factors—barring exceptional circumstances—could not be the basis for departing below the sentencing guidelines' range. Upward departures, however, were authorized for a number of particularly onerous reasons, such as crimes that entailed extreme physical or psychological injury or loss of life.

This brand-new sentencing regime took effect November 1, 1987, and was the law I was bound to apply when I took office exactly seven years later. During the next ten years, I was significantly hemmed in by the mandatory nature of the sentencing guidelines.

In 2005, the Supreme Court rendered its opinion in *United States v. Booker.* In this landmark decision, the majority of the justices ruled that it was unconstitutional for Congress to have required that the sentencing guidelines be mandatory. It recognized Congress's laudatory desire in 1984—when it put in place its mandatory sentencing regime—to eliminate sentencing disparity, but reasoned that it could not constitutionally preclude the judges from exercising their discretion within any statutorily created maximum and minimum term.

The Supreme Court, therefore, made the guidelines advisory. The judges were now permitted, and indeed required, to consider the previously proscribed individual characteristics of the defendant—in addition to the nature of the crime—as a basis for imposing a sentence outside the guidelines' range. The circuit courts of appeal could only disagree with the sentencing judge's out-of-guidelines sentence if it was procedurally defective, such as below a mandatory minimum, or basically substantively off the wall.

But what about the jurors' role? They have nothing to do with sentencing except in very few situations. Once they decide that a defendant is guilty, it is the judge who has the sole power to determine the facts and circumstances that will drive the sentence. The Fitch case is a stark example of just how powerful that power is.

In sentencing Fitch to about twenty-two years—even though the sentencing range for the crimes for which he was convicted was forty-one to fifty-one months—Judge Mahan believed that an upward departure was warranted because he determined that "the death of Maria Bozi was the means that Mr. Fitch used to effectuate the offenses of which he was found guilty." That issue was never before the jury. But once the jury found him guilty of bank fraud, Judge Mahan had the power to decide that Fitch killed his wife and to sentence him accordingly. This is because the Supreme Court ruled a number of years ago that the sentencing judge can consider facts that a jury cannot—and the judge can even find those facts by a lesser standard than proof beyond a reasonable doubt.

Thus, the judge can increase the defendant's sentence based—as in Fitch's case—on uncharged conduct and even for acquitted conduct. In coming to this seemingly counterintuitive conclusion, the high court reasoned that such increases "do not punish a defendant for crimes of which he was not convicted, but rather increase his sentence because of the manner in which he committed the crime of conviction." In respect to acquittals, double jeopardy is not implicated because, as the Supreme Court has explained, "an acquittal is not a finding of any fact." Thus, it "does not prove that the defendant is innocent," and "it is impossible to know exactly why a jury found a defendant not guilty on a certain charge."

Except where Congress has established mandatory minimum punishments, the sentencing judge's power is still the case today. The only constitutional limitation on this enormous power is that Judge Mahan, for example, could not sentence Fitch beyond the maximums that Congress had established for the crimes for which he was convicted. They included, in addition to the bank fraud, a variety of other relatively minor crimes, such as the fraudulent use of an access device and money laundering. Collectively, these other crimes also carried high maximums. When stacked together, which the sentencing judge could do, the total maximum range came to an astonishing 360 years. This was the outer limit of Judge Mahan's sentencing authority. The practical upshot of it all was that Fitch's fate—once convicted of the minor crimes—was totally in the hands of the judge.

Of course, there had to be a factual basis for the judge's determination that Fitch had indeed murdered his wife in order to carry out his bank fraud and credit card crimes. And in fixing the precise sentence, the judge had to consider—under the applicable post-*Booker* advisory guidelines regime—the individual characteristics of the defendant. But even there, Judge Mahan had boundless discretion. He could obtain information upon which to make his findings and fix the term of imprisonment from any reliable source, such as presentence reports prepared by probation officers, which draw on information concerning every aspect of a defendant's life.

Justice Hugo Black explained the rationale for all this when he wrote the majority opinion for the Supreme Court back in 1949 in *Williams v. People of the State of New York*:

> A sentencing judge . . . is not confined to the narrow issue of guilt. His task within fixed statutory or constitutional limits is to determine the type and extent of punishment after the issue of guilt has been determined. And modern concepts of individualizing punishment have made it all the more necessary that a sentencing judge not be denied an opportunity to obtain pertinent information by a requirement of rigid adherence to restrictive rules of evidence properly applicable to the trial.

The *Williams* case stands as a stark example of the power of a sentencing judge to even override a jury's determination. A New York State jury found the defendant guilty of murder in the first degree—which qualified back then for the imposition of the death penalty—but unanimously recommended a life sentence. Relying on the additional information that the trial judge obtained through the court's probation department, the judge sentenced Williams to death. The high court approved by a seven to two vote, thereby setting a precedent for allowing a sentencing judge to consider information not before the jury in deciding whether a defendant should be executed.

Justice Murphy's dissenting opinion cogently articulated the opposite view:

> I agree with the Court as to the value and humaneness of liberal use of probation reports as developed by modern penologists, but, in a capital case, against the unanimous recommendation of a jury, where the report would concededly not have been admissible at the trial, and was not subject to examination by the defendant, I am forced to conclude that the high commands of due process were not obeyed.

I personally agree with Justice Murphy's opinion, but it remains to this day the minority view of the Supreme Court. Its decision in *Williams* regrettably paved the way for states to adopt legislation to allow a trial judge to override a jury's recommendation against the death penalty. Currently, only Alabama, Florida, and Delaware have such laws on the books. But nobody in Delaware is on death row because of override, and it has been fifteen years since a Florida judge has exercised override to impose the ultimate penalty.

Not so in Alabama. In a searing article appearing in the November 17, 2014, issue of the *New Yorker,* it was reported that "[i]n thirty-one of the past thirty-two years, Alabama's judges have condemned someone to death through override at least once." As documented in the article, the Alabama judges' penchant for disregarding a jury's decision against invocation of the death penalty is palpable:

> Nearly seventy Alabama judges have single-handedly ordered an inmate's execution, and collectively they have done so more than a hundred times. Thirty-six of the nearly two hundred convicts on death row are there because of override.

Fortunately, there is no federal law that allows a federal judge to override a jury's verdict against the imposition of the death penalty in the statutes where Congress has put the death penalty in play—such as murder in aid of racketeering, terrorism-related murders, and the like. But, as in *Fitch,* as long as the sentencing judge does not exceed the high maximum sentences that Congress has invariably fixed, the judge's sentencing discretion is enormous.

Judge Mahan made six specific findings to support his conclusion that "Mr. Fitch caused Ms. Bozi's death" and that "the death of Maria Bozi was the means that Mr. Fitch used to effectuate the offenses of which he was found guilty": (1) he failed to report her disappearance to the police; (2) he told different stories to different people about her whereabouts; (3) he tried to sell her clothing and personal effects; (4) he remarried shortly after her disappearance without first seeking a divorce; (5) he had possession of her checkbook, credit cards, and other personal information that any person would have on their person; and (6) he raided her bank account and credit cards by either disguises or forgeries. The judge believed these findings were supported by clear and convincing evidence from the trial testimony and undisputed facts contained in the probation department's presentence report.

The judge then settled on a fifteen-level upward departure, which upped the sentencing range of 41 to 51 months to 210 to 262 months, and sentenced Fitch to the upper limit. Fitch then appealed. Because his case came from the Nevada federal district court, his appeal would be before a panel of three judges for the Ninth Circuit Court of Appeals. And I was one of those judges.

I remember the last time I argued a case before a circuit court of appeals prior to becoming a judge. I was representing the owner of a nursing home who had been found guilty of numerous health violations. My first wife came to the court to listen to my pitch before the three-judge panel sitting up above. I thought I did a pretty good job, and the judges reserved decision after I finished. As I was walking out of the courtroom, Estelle asked me how I thought I did. I told her I wasn't sure, but I was certain of one thing: I would never be sitting up there.

Obviously, I was wrong. In July 1994, I was nominated by President Clinton to fill a vacancy on the federal district court for the Eastern District of New York; in September, I was confirmed by the U.S. Senate, and on October 31—Halloween—I walked into the Brooklyn federal courthouse and put my judicial costume on for the first time.

Before the nomination, I had to be interviewed by the FBI, the Justice Department, and a number of Bar Association Judicial Screening Committees. It was pretty intense stuff. A number of times I was asked if I thought I would have good judicial temperament and be a fair sentencer. I thought it was a silly question because no one would say that he or she would be intemperate and unfair. But I wanted to give a more thoughtful answer than simply saying yes. So I recounted the story of the young adventurer in Joseph Conrad's classic book Lord Jim. *He couldn't wait for the first test of his courage at sea. He was sure that he would be brave and fearless. But when the moment came, he caved. Like Lord Jim, I said that I, too, hoped that I would perform well, but like that young man, I would not know for sure until I was tested.*

Darryl Fulton was my first test. I gave him twenty years. I played it safe. It was right in the middle of the guidelines' range. I couldn't get reversed, and no one could accuse me of being one of those knee-jerk liberal "lenient" sentencers. Looking back, I would have probably given him a below-guidelines sentence today. Even though Booker *had not then been decided, I still had some sentencing discretion to depart from the guidelines range if a totality of permissible factors were present. And Fulton may have qualified for a sentence significantly less than twenty years. He had a tragic upbringing and was handicapped. He was not a violent person; he never hurt anyone. And he was super smart. He decided—as was his right—to be his own lawyer. He probably thought the jury would be sympathetic to him as he hobbled around the courtroom on his one leg. He was articulate, knowledgeable about the law, and had perfect courtroom demeanor. If he had chosen a different path—other than earning his living by robbing banks—he had the talent to be sitting where I was.*

Because the Ninth Circuit is so large, it has four courthouses. They are in Seattle, Portland, San Francisco, and Pasadena. Appeals from Nevada go to San Francisco. In the fall of 2010, I was asked by the circuit court clerk's office if I could sit as a visiting judge to hear three days of appeals in the spring of 2011 in San Francisco. I was happy to say yes. All the Ninth Circuit federal courthouses are first-class facilities, but my favorite is the one in San Francisco. It is a magnificently restored nineteenth-century massive landmark building that was one of the few that survived the infamous 1906 earthquake. The rich mahogany panels of the three courtrooms, the marble floors and walls of the beautiful corridors, and the antique elevator make the building very special. It is open to the public—as are all federal courthouses. It should be on everyone's "must see" list.

The clerk's office tends to the administrative task of calendaring all the appeals. Its policy and practice is to randomly select the three-judge panels and to randomly assign the appeals to the judges. On average, there are about six appeals heard each day a panel sits. I agreed to sit for three consecutive days, and Fitch was one of the appeals randomly assigned to me.

Before the appeals are heard, all the judges are responsible for familiarizing themselves with the trial record and reading the appellate briefs. The judge who has been assigned the appeal has the additional responsibility of preparing a detailed memorandum and recommendation for distribution to his fellow judges.

Unless the judges decide that the case is of little merit and can be summarily disposed of on the briefs, the lawyers are given the opportunity to appear before the panel for oral argument. Based upon the perceived complexity of the case, both sides are usually given between ten and twenty minutes to make their points. The lawyers are invariably questioned by the judges to get to the heart of the issues. The Fitch appeal was obviously one that merited oral argument, and I jumped at the opportunity to question the government's lawyer, Gregory Damm, as to why Fitch was not prosecuted for murder. His responses to my questioning were illuminating:

> **MR. DAMM:** I always hoped that we would find Maria Bozi's body to put some closure to this case. But as you well know, in

the federal government we have a limited jurisdiction to charge violent crimes, in this case murder. We don't know exactly where Mr. Fitch disposed of Maria Bozi's body. We had some belief that he rented a boat and dumped her body in Lake Mead. We had some belief that he went to the Grand Canyon to some remote area . . .

JUDGE BLOCK: You don't need the body to bring a murder charge against him.

MR. DAMM: No, but you need venue, and we didn't have venue. We don't know that she was murdered on a federal enclave.

JUDGE BLOCK: What comes out in the wash is that you couldn't get him for murder directly, so in effect you got him indirectly for murder, right?

MR. DAMM: We certainly did.

Gregory Damm was probably right about the lack of federal venue, but I wondered why Fitch could not have been prosecuted before a jury for murder in the Nevada state court. Upon reflection, I should have asked him that question out of curiosity, but it really made no difference. Under the law, the government had the power to simply prosecute Fitch in federal court for the bank and credit card frauds—which are federal crimes. It did not have to run the risk of prosecuting him in state court before a jury for murder to put him behind bars for decades. It could simply leave it up to the sentencing judge in the federal case to do this "indirectly."

New judges are sent within weeks to a one-week crash course, appropriately referred to as Baby Judges' school. Its primary purpose is to educate the judge about sentencing. The faculty is first-rate. They are usually probation officers who know everything about sentencing.

I was one of sixteen new judges being trained. Our teacher, Rusty Burgess, was a crackerjack. He was a veritable sentencing whiz and drilled us on every aspect of the sentencing laws. At the end of the week, we knew how to go about making the requisite sentencing guidelines calculations.

*While Rusty acknowledged that there was some wiggle room in the then pre-*Booker *regime to render a below-guidelines sentence in extraordinary circumstances, he impressed upon the new judges that this was a relatively rare thing and ran the risk of having the sentence reversed by the appellate court. Playing it safe was the prudent thing, and a sentence within the guidelines range was the way to go. After all, no new judge relished getting reversed.*

Those were the thoughts that were dancing in my head when I sentenced Darryl Fulton shortly after I returned from Baby Judges' school. And it was at Baby Judges' school that I learned that I had the power to hold a convicted criminal accountable for uncharged and acquitted conduct. Whether or not I agreed with that was irrelevant. I was duty-bound to follow the law.

After all the oral arguments that day, I met with the other two panel judges in a conference room near the courtroom to discuss the cases. We voted on each one and decided whether any of them merited a lengthy, full-blown written opinion or whether they could be disposed of in a short memorandum. We believed that *Fitch* warranted a written opinion, and I was assigned the task of writing it.

I started my opinion by commenting that "[b]ecause Fitch has never been charged with his wife's murder, his sentence is a poignant example of a drastic upward departure from the guidelines range—albeit below the statutory maximum—based on uncharged criminal conduct." Nonetheless, even though I recognized that the court "had not had occasion to address a scenario quite like this," I believed that under the law, we were "constrained" to uphold Judge Mahan's decision.

The opinion then tracked the key decisions of the Supreme Court, concluding that it "remains the law that the sentencing judge has the power to sentence a defendant based upon facts not found by a jury up to the statutory maximum, and that 'the defendant has no right to a jury determination of the facts that the judge deems relevant.'" I explained that "[t]he only restrictions that the Supreme Court has imposed on a district court's power to impose a sentence less than the statutory maximum are that the sentence must not be tainted by procedural error, and that it must not be substantively unreasonable."

Fitch's appellate lawyer had principally argued that his sentence was procedurally defective because there was no "clear and convincing evidence" that Fitch murdered Bozi; in any event, drastically departing from the advisory guidelines range for the crimes of which Fitch was convicted was substantively unreasonable. I rejected both contentions.

In doing so, I agreed with Fitch's lawyer that "clear and convincing" was indeed the requisite burden of proof—although not as high as the "proof beyond a reasonable doubt" standard if the jury had to determine if Fitch killed Bozi. I explained, however, that an appellate court must give significant deference to the findings of a trial judge and that "[i]n order to reverse a district court's factual findings as clearly erroneous, we must determine that the district court's factual findings were illogical, implausible, or without support in the record." This was not the case. As I recounted:

> The district court was confronted with a defendant who had failed to report his wife's disappearance, gave several inconsistent—and in light of his possession of her passport, implausible—statements as to her whereabouts, and tried to dispose of her clothes and personal effects. He then used her bank account, credit cards, and health insurance—sometimes through forgery and deception—and eventually married a former girlfriend while still ostensibly married to his missing wife. It was eminently reasonable for the district court to infer that Bozi was dead, that Fitch knew she was dead, and that he had brought about her death in order to pillage her assets.

And I concluded that the sentence was legally correct because it did not exceed the huge maximums for the crimes for which Fitch was convicted—at least 360 months—and was substantively reasonable because the 262 months sentence "was well short of the guidelines range for both first-degree murder (life) and second-degree murder (324 to 405 months) for someone in Fitch's criminal history category."

I wondered, however, whether my decision would have been different if Judge Mahan had sentenced Fitch within the guideline range for second degree murder, which covers any malicious killing. I suppose I would have had no choice since putting someone behind bars for at least 324 months (the low end of the guidelines range) for killing his wife can hardly be viewed as unreasonable. And I also wondered whether I would have made the same call as Judge Mahan if I were the sentencing judge. I think I would have. Every bit of evidence and uncontested information convinced me that Fitch must have killed his wife. And I might have sentenced him to more than 262 months. In effect, Judge Mahan cut Fitch a break by sentencing him to about five years less than the minimum warranted under the guidelines for second-degree murder.

Unfortunately, my opinion did not dissuade Judge Goodwin from dissenting. He did not agree with Judge Smith and myself that there was clear and convincing evidence that Fitch murdered his wife because "[w]e simply do not know any of the circumstances of Bozi's disappearance." Of course, I thought that my opinion effectively explained why we had to affirm Judge Mahan's decision, and I suspect that Judge Goodwin just wasn't comfortable with acknowledging the harshness of the law that allows a single human being—although a judge—to convict a person for an uncharged crime (and even by a lesser standard than proof beyond a reasonable doubt), especially one as serious as murder.

I believe that Judge Mahan was perfectly competent to decide that David Fitch murdered Maria Bozi, but I do wonder—as I suspect Judge Goodwin does as well—what is left to that quaint notion of trial by jury?

2

Acquitted Criminal Conduct

Anthony Praddy and the Raleigh Place Crew

The Crime

With a firm understanding of the power and responsibility of the sentencing judge, we are ready to delve into a wide array of challenging sentencing decisions I have had to make throughout my years on the bench. I have decided to start with the *Praddy* case because—like Judge Mahan in the *Fitch* case—it was now my turn to decide whether to hold a defendant accountable for murder. On April 1, 2004, Detective Selwyn Fonrose, a New York City police officer patrolling a drug-infested neighborhood in Brooklyn, made eye contact with sixteen-year-old Anthony Praddy, who then—according to the officer—threw a bag of marijuana on the street. Praddy ran into 16 Raleigh Place, where his grandmother lived. The officer apprehended him and pulled from Praddy's knapsack twenty-seven small bags of marijuana and a loaded .25-caliber Jennings revolver with a defaced serial number. Praddy was arrested on the spot. He ultimately pleaded guilty to criminal possession of a loaded firearm and on March 7, 2006, was sentenced in state court to one year behind bars. Before then, he was free on supervised release.

On May 26, 2004, less than two months after Praddy had been arrested, Kevon Simon—another teenager—was shot to death outside a barbershop on Church Avenue, around the corner from Raleigh Place. The police were not then able to discover who murdered Simon, and it became a "cold case."

On June 18, 2009 (about two years after Praddy had served his time on the state gun charge and about five years after Simon had been murdered), the feds arrested Praddy, known as "Birdman," and two of his buddies—Kiond Jones and Terrell "Terror" Whyte—for a number of drug-related crimes involving the sale and conspiracy to sell large quantities of marijuana between 1998 and 2009; they were also charged with using guns in furtherance of the drug conspiracy.

I will never forget the date: June 4, 1969. I had just finished eating dinner when the phone rang. I was feeling pretty chipper as I picked it up; it was a beautiful night, and I had settled a nice negligence case that day that netted a $10,000 fee. It was not big by today's standards, but for a solo practitioner in the early stages of his legal career, it was big for me. On the other end of the phone was a state trooper from Woodstock, which would soon become the famous place for the drug-pervaded festival that brought thousands of young people to this upstate New York town to hear the likes of Jimi Hendrix and Janis Joplin wail away. He asked me if Sheldon Block was my brother. I said he was. He told me that he had killed himself the night before. The preliminary investigation indicated that he had been high on LSD, had plunged a knife into his stomach, and bled to death.

Sheldon was thirty-nine when he died. He was a kind, sensitive, artistic person who was probably not meant for this world. His passion was his art, but he had never sold any of his paintings and had no will to support himself. My parents paid for a little studio apartment in Woodstock, which was an artists' community, where he lived on the small amount of money they gave him. He devoted himself to painting abstract images of amazing colors. He had told me he only saw them when he was on LSD. He was a disciple of the guru Timothy Leary, the Harvard professor who extolled the mind-altering virtues of that drug.

I don't think Sheldon committed suicide. My sense is that he stabbed himself while he was tripping on the drug and was not in his right mind.

I think of Sheldon whenever I have a drug case.

Praddy, Jones, and Whyte were arraigned by a magistrate judge. Every person arrested for a crime must be promptly arraigned before a judicial officer. The purpose of an arraignment is to publicly advise the defendant of the charges against him, to ask whether he pleads "guilty" or "not guilty," and if "not guilty" to fix bail pending trial. Because Jones and Whyte had many prior brushes with the law and couldn't make bail, they were detained. Although Praddy had spent a year in jail on the gun charge, he otherwise had a clean record, and Magistrate Judge Gold set bail at $100,000 with an unsecured bond signed by his parents, meaning that he could remain free pending trial.

But the feds had reason to believe that Praddy killed Simon. Tellingly, they had interviewed another one of his buddies, Hayden McQuilkin, after McQuilkin was arrested by the NYPD in June 2006 for illegally reentering the country. They learned that McQuilkin had snuck back into the United States in 2002 after having been previously convicted—and deported to Trinidad—for selling drugs.

McQuilkin's lawyer believed that the government would give him a cooperation deal and spare him from once again being deported because he had important information to disclose about what was happening in the Raleigh Place neighborhood.

He was right. McQuilkin told the federal agents that after he came back into the country, he resumed selling drugs there. He implicated a bunch of other Raleigh Place drug sellers, including Praddy. But he went one step further. He told the government that he witnessed Praddy shoot Kevon Simon.

The feds were hesitant to charge Praddy with the murder at that time based upon the word of just one witness, especially one who was a criminal in his own right. However, on April 17, 2010—about ten months after Praddy and his codefendants had been indicted on the drug charges and about five months before that trial was to start—Raymond Dowdie was arrested by the NYPD on a firearm charge. He had previously been arrested on immigration charges in 2004 and deported to Jamaica. He returned illegally in 2007, lived in Florida for some time, and eventually made his way back to New York City before his arrest.

As with McQuilkin, Dowdie's lawyer thought that Dowdie should come clean and cut a cooperation deal with the government. When the feds heard what Dowdie had to say, they jumped. Dowdie disclosed detailed information regarding the inner workings of the Raleigh Place Crew and the identities of its members—including Praddy, Jones, and Whyte—the commission of multiple acts of violence by them and other Crew members, and the identifies of victims and witnesses.

Raymond Dowdie also told the feds that a few days after Simon was murdered, Praddy told him that he was the one who killed him. The murder case was now out of cold storage.

With two critical cooperators in tow, on July 22, 2010, the government superseded its original indictment against Praddy, Jones, and Whyte and charged them with a host of new crimes under the Racketeer Influenced and Corrupt Organizations Act, better known as the RICO Act. In that indictment, Kiond Jones was also charged with attempting to murder Moses Osborne and kidnapping—with Dowdie—Craig Hecclewood, two rival drug pushers. And Anthony Praddy was charged with murdering Simon.

The indictment alleged that the acts of violence were part of a pattern of racketeering activity by Jones, Praddy, and Whyte as members of the Raleigh Place Crew. If the jury convicted them of committing these violent crimes, either as part of their racketeering activity or—in Praddy's case—in aid of racketeering, they would face long terms of imprisonment. As for Praddy, I would have no choice under the law but to sentence him to jail for the rest of his life for the murder of Kevon Simon.

RICO was enacted by Congress in 1970. Coming on the heels of *The Godfather*, its avowed goal was to put the mob out of business. Congress pulled no punches. It was blunt in declaring that the purpose of the act was "to seek the eradication of organized crime in the United States."

The principal way in which RICO sought to do this was by focusing on patterns of criminal behavior rather than on individual crimes. It did this by creating the concept of a criminal "enterprise." Once you were found to be a member of a criminal enterprise, you could be convicted of racketeering under RICO if twice within a decade you engaged in any of a broad range of criminal activities—including murder, robbery, extortion, bribery, and (as in Praddy's case) the distribution of drugs—that were part of the common goal of generating money for, or increasing your status in, the enterprise. These were traditionally state crimes, but with RICO, Congress provided the hook to make them federal racketeering crimes so long as the affairs of the enterprise had any effect upon interstate commerce—which, like taking someone's money or simply using the telephone, was easy to establish.

RICO authorized heavy prison sentences. It also carried a deadly economic punch. Convicted defendants would have to forfeit all of their ill-gotten gains, including all proceeds from the enterprise's activities. They would also be subject to treble damages for any monies they took from their victims.

Membership in a Mafia family would be the textbook example of being part of a criminal enterprise. Before the passage of RICO, the government's efforts against the mobs were piecemeal. It attacked isolated segments of the criminal organization as its members engaged in single criminal acts. The leaders, when caught, were only penalized for what seemed to be unimportant crimes. The larger meaning of these crimes was lost because the big picture would not be presented in a single criminal prosecution. With the passage of the act, the entire picture of the organization's criminal behavior and the involvement of all those associated with the enterprise could be captured.

Thus, RICO could be employed to wipe out an entire criminal organization by rounding up and prosecuting its members in a handful of criminal prosecutions. It was designed, therefore, to put gangsters behind bars—for long periods—and to attack the underbelly of a criminal enterprise by taking both its leaders and their "family" off the streets in one fell swoop. The typical Mafia racketeering prosecution would thus have multiple defendants. Once they were linked to a Mafia family, it was relatively easy to convict them of racketeering. For example, if threats were made by a mobster over the telephone on just two occasions over a ten-year period to collect a debt for his criminal enterprise, he would be guilty of not only making the threats, but also of the more serious crime of racketeering.

While RICO has been successfully employed against the Mafia crime families, the federal government has also used it to attack gangs, such as the Bloods, Crypts, and Latin Kings. The Raleigh Place Crew were mainly Bloods who had cornered the marijuana drug market in that area, and the government deployed RICO to break up the Crew and get it off the streets.

Although a magistrate judge handled the arraignment on the initial indictment, in light of the superseding indictment, the three defendants now had to be arraigned again. I did it this time. I had set the original case down for trial for the second week of September and had to decide if that trial date would hold in light of the new charges. I also had to decide whether Praddy should remain at liberty pending trial because he was now being charged with murder.

The new arraignment took place on July 22, 2010, two days after the superseding indictment had been rendered. Each of the defendant's lawyers entered a "not guilty" plea for his client. None of the lawyers asked that the trial date be changed, and the focus then shifted to whether I should revoke Praddy's bail and have him join his codefendants in jail. Praddy's lawyer, Mitchell Dinnerstein, unabashedly told me that it would be "a terrible thing to do."

Mitch Dinnerstein was assigned to represent Praddy, who could not afford to retain a lawyer. In addition to his private practice, Dinnerstein was a member of the court's select panel of qualified lawyers under the Criminal Justice Act (CJA), which requires each of the country's federal district courts to ensure that competent criminal defense lawyers are assigned to represent indigent defendants. Dinnerstein had been qualified to be a member of the court's panel of CJA lawyers, and deservedly so. He enjoyed a reputation as a highly skilled and resourceful criminal defense lawyer who passionately represented his clients and ensured they got a fair trial.

The Eastern District of New York takes great pride in the quality of the court's CJA lawyers, as I suspect all federal district courts do. They are the unsung heroes of the criminal justice system. Although they currently get paid $125 per hour for their services from the government, it is small change compared to what the hot-shot private lawyers make for representing mafiosi and other well-heeled clients.

Although each district court has a federally funded federal defender's office that is charged with representing indigent criminal defendants, they are often understaffed and can't take care of all the business. Moreover, when there are multiple defendants—as in the Praddy case—the office is conflicted out; it can't represent them all. CJA lawyers must therefore be assigned to fill the void. They are essential to the functioning of the criminal justice system.

Because indigent defendants get a lawyer free of charge, they often believe the old adage that "you get what you pay for." Nothing could be further from the truth. The federal defenders and CJA lawyers are among the best. Since they are always in court and try a great many cases, they are highly skilled and experienced. They can go toe-to-toe with the prosecutors and the best of the criminal defense bar. And, because of the volume of work they handle, they are particularly knowledgeable about sentencing. I often comment that if I ever had to be sentenced, I would prefer to be represented by a federal defender or CJA lawyer.

Mitch Dinnerstein would be high on my list. What I particularly like about him is that he is not afraid to take on the judge. But his zeal can sometimes try the judge's patience. Mitch believed passionately that

Praddy was only a kid who had occasionally sold small quantities of marijuana, that he was not engaged in racketeering, and that he did not murder Kevon Simon. Tensions between us started to mount from the get-go, and as events unfolded, they would reach tsunami proportions.

The government asked me at the re-arraignment to send Praddy to jail pending trial because he was now being charged with racketeering and murder. This was contrary to the recommendation of the Pretrial Services officer who had been supervising Praddy during the past year while he was out on bail. He recounted that Praddy had behaved well and did not believe it was necessary to have him sit in jail before the trial. While the prosecutor usually does not take issue with the government's Pretrial Services' recommendation, it did so here. The lead prosecutor, Seth DuCharme, believed that the landscape had significantly changed because the government now had telling evidence that Praddy murdered Simon. Without naming McQuilkin or Dowdie, DuCharme stated that "we have an eyewitness to the murder who saw Mr. Praddy shoot the victim Kevon Simon to death, and we have a witness who heard Mr. Praddy make admissions."

I decided to flush this out and required the agent in charge of the case to testify that afternoon at what I then deemed to be a bail revocation hearing. Under the law, before I could revoke bail, I had to consider a number of factors, including the nature of the charges and the risk of flight, the weight of the evidence, the history and characteristics of the defendant, and the danger to the community if the defendant was not incarcerated. But because of the murder charge, the defense had the burden of overcoming a presumption that remand was required.

After listening to Agent Robert Foy testify about the events leading to the murder indictment, I stated that "given the seriousness of the charge, there's such a heightened motivation to flee here, I feel a remand is indicated." DuCharme was obviously pleased with my comment, but mindful that the trial would begin in just three months, he added "given the posture of the defendant, the timing of the trial, the potential prejudice to him, if any, by a short term of incarceration, given the risk of flight . . ." Before he could finish his sentence, Dinnerstein, his face reddening, swung into action, and things got heated between us:

DINNERSTEIN: "If any"? Did he say "if any"? How would he like to spend two months in jail? That is an outrageous thing for him to say, "if any."

THE COURT: Now that you've said that, he is remanded.

DINNERSTEIN: That is not fair.

THE COURT: Before I remand you. Just relax.

DINNERSTEIN: All right. Remand me first. Your Honor, please let me finish.

THE COURT: You have spoken.

DINNERSTEIN: No, I have not spoken. I have not spoken, Your Honor, because this person, the probation officer, has known him for thirteen months. These charges have been at least on the table since November of 2009. He's known him for thirteen months.

THE COURT: He will be exonerated in a couple of months' time.

DINNERSTEIN: He is going to be in jail for two months and you know, blessedly, Your Honor, it is so much more difficult for me to defend him when he is in jail than when he is not in jail.

THE COURT: How much time do you want to vent your spleen? You are yelling, screaming. You are a professional lawyer.

DINNERSTEIN: I won't yell and scream.

THE COURT: The softer you speak, the easier it is for me to digest things and possibly rule in your favor. I am just telling you in the realistic world how it works. I am not going to remand him because of your enthusiastic support of your client. I am not going to remand him because his parents are not wealthy people. I am simply remanding him because in my judgment there's a very, very heightened risk of flight simply because of the fact that these charges have actually been leveled against him now. I tried to explore, you know, the questioning of the Agent. I tried to conduct a proceeding that smacks of fairness for me to reflect upon whether there's a good faith basis for these charges. . . .

DINNERSTEIN: I understand the seriousness of the charge, Your Honor, and the reason possibly that I am getting indignant is because I have known him also for thirteen months.

THE COURT: The world is not going to come to an end.

DINNERSTEIN: For him, spending two months in jail is a very serious matter.

As Dinnerstein continued to make an impassioned pitch for his client's freedom, I realized that it was improvident for me to have said, "Now that you've said that, he is remanded," after Dinnerstein verbally attacked DuCharme for arguing that the "potential prejudice" for Praddy was not significant because he would only be in jail for two months before the trial. I would never penalize a client because of a lawyer's comments or behavior, but unless you were in the courtroom at that time you could not appreciate Dinnerstein's raging tone and mannerisms. I momentarily lost my cool. I counted to ten, took a deep breath, gained my composure, and wrapped up the hearing by allowing Dinnerstein to make one last pitch—and agreeing that DuCharme's comment was "a wrong thing to say." I then rendered my final decision.

THE COURT: Mr. Dinnerstein, I have a tough job and I don't like to put people in jail, but I'm remanding him, and in September he will be able to be exonerated with your careful and capable defense. We will see how it goes, all right, but that is my decision.

I thought we were through, but Dinnerstein was not finished. "Wait a minute," he called out. "Mr. Praddy would like to say something."

It's unusual for this to happen. I am sure that Dinnerstein, as a skilled lawyer, must have cautioned his client that whatever he said could come back to haunt him if he said anything that could possibly incriminate him. But I thought that Praddy had the right to speak.

Everyone in the courtroom was glued to their seats as Praddy slowly got up and timidly walked toward me. I hunched forward from above. It was the first time that I truly fixed my eyes on him. I was struck by his slight, frail build and his small stature—I estimated that he was about five foot four. He softly blurted out, "I go to probation every week. Can I be under house arrest?"

I wondered whether he really understood the seriousness of the charges he faced and did not change my decision. As he was being led out of the courtroom, he asked me whether he could have a minute with his family. I told him that "I will leave it to the marshals. You are under their control." I didn't wait to see what they would do.

As I got off the bench and left the courtroom, I wondered whether Dinnerstein might be right—that Praddy was indeed just a kid who was occasionally selling dope on the streets and had nothing to do with the murder of Kevon Simon. Only time—and the jury's verdict after the trial—would tell us.

I picked the jury on September 20, and the trial started two days later. As is common in the Eastern District of New York—unlike most other places in the country—the jury was a fairly typical diverse mix of blacks, whites, and Hispanics.

Shortly before the trial, I determined that "Terror" Whyte could not be tried together with his codefendants due to the existence of a potential conflict with his attorney. He would eventually work out a plea deal with the government and plead guilty to some of the charges against him. The trial would therefore proceed only against Praddy and Jones.

Not surprisingly, the two cooperators, McQuilkin and Dowdie, were the principal witnesses for the prosecution and gave the most damning testimony. Dowdie acknowledged that he became the leader of the Crew in the mid-1990s and identified about a dozen persons appointed by him who worked with him through the next several years, including Jones, Praddy, and Praddy's cousin Lindsey. Collectively, they sold "thousands of pounds" of marijuana in the Raleigh Place area from the mid-1990s until mid-2009.

Dowdie testified that Jones was one of Dowdie's "lieutenants," and Praddy was one of the "workers." Dowdie also explained that the crew considered Raleigh Place to be their exclusive turf and "interlopers were run . . . off the block." As an example, he testified about having pistol-whipped an interloper as punishment for selling on the block.

McQuilkin also acknowledged his culpability. He testified that the Crew worked in shifts and that Jones and Praddy were members of shift teams. As he explained: "From six in the morning till ten, right, Dre will work. After he finished, then you have it could be Lindsey and Birdman come on that day, it could be Kiond and D, Devon come on that day. It could be Josh and somebody else or it could be one of them by himself."

Tellingly, McQuilkin testified that he himself bought marijuana from Praddy; he saw other people buying marijuana from him; he saw Praddy selling marijuana four to five times a week in Raleigh Place. He also saw Praddy with Dowdie, Kiond, and numerous others, most of whom Dowdie had identified as members of the Crew. In sum, McQuilkin saw Praddy and Kiond selling marijuana together "[l]ike four, five times a week" at "[e]very week, selling marijuana hundreds of times. . . . Hundreds," he said, was "not an exaggeration."

But the government did not have to rely just on McQuilkin's testimony about Praddy's drug dealings. After he was picked up in 2006 and became a cooperator, McQuilkin agreed to wear a wire, and the government put into evidence audio- and videotaped recordings of Praddy selling marijuana to McQuilkin on two occasions in 2007 and two more in 2008—the most recent being on September 4, 2008, just months before Praddy was arrested. There was also a video of Praddy buying marijuana from someone else in 2007.

But the most dramatic part of McQuilkin's testimony was his account of Kevon Simon's murder. He testified, in response to DuCharme's questioning, that he walked into a bodega to buy cigarettes and saw Simon—who was known as Belize—in the store. Praddy and cousin Lindsey then came in and Lindsey said to Belize, "Didn't I tell you don't be selling no fucking weed on this block?" Belize in turn said, "Yo, fuck you, man. Get the fuck out of my face." McQuilkin then left the bodega.

As DuCharme continued to question him, McQuilkin testified about what happened next:

> **DUCHARME:** What were you doing outside the store?
>
> **MCQUILKIN:** Smoking my cigarette.
>
> **DUCHARME:** What did you observe while you were smoking your cigarette?
>
> **MCQUILKIN:** Belize came out. He walked inside the barbershop.
>
> **DUCHARME:** I'm showing you what is in evidence as Government's Exhibit 438. Do you recognize that?
>
> **MCQUILKIN:** Yes, sir.
>
> **DUCHARME:** What is that?
>
> **MCQUILKIN:** That's the barbershop.
>
> **DUCHARME:** Now, when you were outside smoking your cigarette, did you observe Birdman and Lindsey do anything?

MCQUILKIN: They went towards Raleigh. I didn't look to see exactly if they turned or—

DUCHARME: They went off towards Raleigh?

MCQUILKIN: Yes, sir.

DUCHARME: What did Belize do?

MCQUILKIN: He went inside the barbershop.

DUCHARME: What did you do next?

MCQUILKIN: Smoked my cigarette. When my cigarette finished, I went in the barbershop with my DVDs trying to sell them.

DUCHARME: What happened once you got inside the barbershop?

MCQUILKIN: I was trying to sell my DVDs.

DUCHARME: Were there other people there?

MCQUILKIN: Yes—Belize, the barber, customers.

DUCHARME: What happened next, Mr. McQuilkin?

MCQUILKIN: Lindsey walks in the barbershop. He says: "Yo, let me talk to you outside."

DUCHARME: Who did he say that to?

MCQUILKIN: Belize.

DUCHARME: After Lindsey walked into the barbershop and said: "Yo, let me talk to you," what did Belize do?

MCQUILKIN: He walked outside behind him.

DUCHARME: What did you do?

MCQUILKIN: I walked outside also.

DUCHARME: And when you got out onto the street, Mr. McQuilkin, tell the jury what you saw.

MCQUILKIN: When I got out to the street, the store would be this way. I went to the left; they went towards the right. So, as I'm walking down, I'm looking back like this (indicating) because I kind of sensed what's going to happen, so I'm looking back. I see Birdman pulls out a gun and fired two times at Belize. In return I ran across the street and I kept running away from there.

DUCHARME: And when you say you saw Birdman, is that the same Birdman you've identified as the defendant in this case?

MCQUILKIN: Yes, sir.

DUCHARME: Could you actually see the gun in his hand, Mr. McQuillan?

MCQUILKIN: Yes, sir.

DUCHARME: Did you see the shots being fired?

MCQUILKIN: I seen the trigger pulled.

McQuilkin then explained why he did not call the police: "Because I had Immigration on me and plus—I didn't want to say it like that—but they some dangerous dudes, you know what I mean, your family around there, you ain't going to tell the police, it's from fear." It was not until two years later, after he was picked up as an illegal alien, that he agreed to become a cooperator and tell all, because he "didn't want to be deported."

Finally, McQuilkin detailed his cooperation agreement with the government. He had agreed to plead guilty to the immigration charge and also pleaded guilty to conspiring to possess with intent to distribute 50 grams or more of cocaine base in exchange for the government agreeing to allow the court to sentence him, in its absolute discretion, to a lesser term of imprisonment than what otherwise might be the case. He acknowledged that by pleading guilty, he was putting himself at the mercy of the court and faced a sentence of life in prison if he did not testify honestly. As he explained, if the government was satisfied with his cooperation, it would:

[w]rite a letter of recommendation to the sentencing—my sentencing judge but with the letter my whole criminal history, everything I told you about my past life here today has to go with the recommendation from them and it's up to the judge to weigh and judge and see if he want to give me any amount of time he choose to give me but it's not up to them [the government] to decide if I get jail time or if I don't.

As for Dowdie's knowledge of the shooting, he testified that sometime after it happened he had a conversation with Lindsey and explained, in response to DuCharme's direct examination, what then transpired:

DUCHARME: And did Lindsey tell you whether or not anything had happened to Belize?

DOWDIE: Yes.

DUCHARME: What did Lindsey tell you happened to Belize?

DOWDIE: Said he got killed.

DUCHARME: After Lindsey told you Belize had been killed, Mr. Dowdie, did you have a conversation with Birdman about the circumstances under which Belize was killed?

DOWDIE: Yes.

DUCHARME: And about how long after Lindsey told you that Belize had been killed did you speak to Birdman?

DOWDIE: A couple of days.

DUCHARME: And where were you when you had this conversation?

DOWDIE: It was on Raleigh Place.

DUCHARME: Were there other people around?

DOWDIE: Yes.

DUCHARME: And, Mr. Dowdie, what did Birdman tell you about the killing of Belize?

DOWDIE: Well, basically, when it happened, we was like when we heard what happened we was joking about it, like, it was like a mistake, whatever, fluke, whatever. So, I asked him what happened. He told me he saw Belize selling and he approached Belize and then it start, they started arguing and that's when he pulled the gun. Belize tried to grab the gun and that's when Belize got shot.

DUCHARME: And who told you this?

DOWDIE: Birdman.

DUCHARME: And is that the same Birdman you identified as a defendant in this courtroom?

DOWDIE: Yes, sir.

Dowdie further told DuCharme that after Praddy shot Belize, he was treated "differently in the group":

DUCHARME: How was he treated differently?

DOWDIE: I would say, like, he put in work, got his weight up.

DUCHARME: What does it mean to "put in work," Mr. Dowdie?

DOWDIE: I would say we were looking at him like Birdman was looking at him like somebody different from what he just did.

DUCHARME: What does it mean to "put in work," Mr. Dowdie?

DOWDIE: Basically to kill somebody.

DUCHARME: What does it mean to "get your weight up"?

DOWDIE: To kill somebody.

Like McQuilkin, Dowdie also testified about his cooperation agreement. On July 16, 2010—just four days prior to the superseding indictment against Praddy, Jones, and Whyte—he pleaded guilty before Magistrate Judge Gold to a separate two-count information. The first count charged him with engaging in racketeering as a member of the Raleigh Place Crew between January 1, 1998, and June 1, 2009. In that regard, he admitted that during that time span he conspired to distribute and possess with intent to distribute one thousand kilograms or more of marijuana and that in May 2002 he kidnapped Craig "Roach" Hecclewood. Like McQuilkin, he also faced life if he did not faithfully cooperate with the government and testify truthfully. And, like McQuilkin, he also hoped that if the government told the court it was satisfied with his cooperation, the sentencing judge would cut him a big break and, possibly, even set him free.

Not surprisingly, Dinnerstein and Jones's lawyer ripped into McQuilkin and Dowdie on cross-examination, hammering home that they could not be believed because they would say anything to save their necks.

The government produced a number of other witnesses, such as the police officer who caught Praddy with the loaded gun and the drugs in his knapsack; the coroner, who testified that Kevon Simon was shot twice, which was consistent with McQuilkin's testimony; and a host of others who told of the Crew selling marijuana in the area of Raleigh Place. But no one, other than McQuilkin and Dowdie, knew who shot Simon.

After the government finished with its direct case, the ball was then in the defendants' court. Under the law, they didn't have to do anything; their lawyers could simply argue to the jury that the government did not prove their clients' guilt by the high standard of "proof beyond a reasonable doubt." And, of course, the defendants did not have to testify. I explained to the jury that under the Constitution, if the defendants chose to stand mute, it could not hold that against them, and no inference of guilt could be drawn.

Jones decided to exercise his constitutional right to remain silent. But, to everyone's surprise, Dinnerstein put his client on the stand. It was a bold move; rarely does it happen. When it does, the defendant can be cross-examined and usually winds up making matters worse.

As Praddy walked, ever so slowly, to the witness stand, I noticed how the jurors started to straighten up and pay rapt attention. This was the big moment in the trial.

Praddy was reasonably composed but spoke so low that I had to tell him to speak up and use the microphone. As I looked at him—only a few feet away from me—he still looked like a kid, and I wondered whether he could really have shot Simon when he was just sixteen years old. But under the law, he could be prosecuted at any time for committing a murder at that tender age.

Dinnerstein first asked him some softball questions. Praddy said that he was born on September 11, 1987; he lived with his father, mother, and sister in Queens; and had last lived on Raleigh Place—at his grandmother's house—in 2003. His parents and grandmother were in court.

Dinnerstein quickly went right to the heart of his client's testimony, and Praddy, not surprisingly, said flat out that he never shot anybody; in fact, he had no knowledge of Simon's murder until he was arrested for killing him. But he did admit to selling marijuana. In light of the video sales to McQuilkin, he really had no choice. He went further, however, and admitted to selling marijuana to McQuilkin "fifteen, twenty times over the years," and that he regularly sold weed on Raleigh Place and the surrounding area from 2003 until he was arrested in 2009. But he marginalized the magnitude of the sales, claiming that it was only "nickel, dime, quarter of ounce" at a time; never amounting to more than $300. "I would bag it up in dimes, so you get—you would get fifteen dimes out of an ounce. That would be $150 profit."

Because of Detective Fonrose's testimony, Dinnerstein also questioned Praddy about being caught with marijuana and the loaded gun in his knapsack in 2004. He denied throwing any bags of marijuana on the ground before Fonrose chased him into his grandmother's house. But he admitted that he did have the gun in the knapsack. Dinnerstein asked the question that the government would undoubtedly ask on cross-examination: "Why did you have a gun on you that day?" Praddy's best answer was, "I'm a kid. I don't know." He denied ever firing the gun or having a gun on any other day.

Just before Dinnerstein finished his direct examination, Praddy testified that he had attended Kingsborough Community College in 2007 and 2008, had worked for Home Depot for a period of time in 2008, and had obtained a welder's license. It was time for DuCharme's cross-examination.

Right off the bat, DuCharme confronted Praddy with the fact that he had previously been arrested back in October 2003 for selling marijuana and had had fifty-four bags on him. While he didn't remember the number of bags, he did acknowledge that "around that time is when I started selling marijuana." All told, he testified to selling only a "couple of pounds" over the years. The government brought out, however, that Praddy had $1,000 of cash on him on the date he was arrested in 2009. Under intensive cross-examination, Praddy testified that "there was no marijuana at all" in his knapsack when he was arrested in 2004—even though the marijuana was introduced into evidence—and said that he just got the loaded gun on the "same day." It was "the only time [he] ever carried a gun in [his] life."

Dinnerstein ended his case by having Praddy's mother testify. She carried herself well, was smartly dressed, and spoke clearly and persuasively. She made a good impression on me. Not surprisingly, she painted her son in a very positive light.

It was time for the lawyers to give their summations.

The government always goes first. After the defendants' lawyers sum up, the government's lawyer is entitled to end the summations with a brief rebuttal.

Andrew Goldsmith gave the government's principal summation. He had ably assisted DuCharme in presenting the government's case. Goldsmith carefully led the jury through the key testimony and evidence against Jones and Praddy. Collectively, they overwhelmingly supported the racketeering and drug charges against them, so Goldsmith decided to end by dramatically focusing on the unsolved murder of Kevon Simon:

> Now, let's talk about Anthony Praddy. Again, Raymond Dowdie and Hayden McQuilkin both told you they saw Praddy carrying a gun. And you know without a doubt that Praddy carried a gun on April 1, 2004, because he told you that himself, from the witness stand. That's the day that Officer Fonrose caught him. You know that Praddy carried the gun that day in support of the marijuana conspiracy, because in addition to the loaded gun in his backpack, he had twenty-seven bags of marijuana.
>
> Now, Praddy testified that he didn't have any marijuana in his backpack that day. He told you that sometimes he had fifteen bags, and sometimes he had thirty bags, but he absolutely never, ever had twenty-seven bags. That's just not believable, ladies and gentlemen.
>
> He also told you that the one day in his entire life that he had a gun just happened to be the day that Officer Fonrose caught him. That's not believable either. Is Anthony Praddy the unluckiest person on earth, ladies and gentlemen? No, he isn't.
>
> Finally, of course, Anthony Praddy carried, he brandished, and fired a firearm when he murdered Kevon Simon, and as we discussed, he did that to protect his and the Raleigh Place Crew's drug territory.
>
> The evidence that you have seen in this trial proves beyond a reasonable doubt that the Raleigh Place Crew dominated Raleigh Place and Church Avenue for a decade, selling thousands of kilograms of marijuana.
>
> It proves beyond a reasonable doubt that on behalf of the crew, Anthony Praddy murdered Kevon Simon, and that on behalf of the crew, Kiond Jones attempted to murder Moses Osborne and kidnapped Craig Hecclewood. I ask you to find the defendants guilty of all charges.

It was Dinnerstein's turn. He acknowledged that his client was guilty of selling small quantities of marijuana to McQuilkin but minimized the amount of drugs that Praddy sold throughout the years and contended that the government did not prove that his client was part of any racketeering enterprise. As for Simon's murder, Dinnerstein threw down the gauntlet: "Do you believe McQuilkin and Dowdie or do you believe what Anthony Praddy says, that he had nothing to do with the murder on the streets of Brooklyn on May 26, 2004?"

After extolling the virtues of his client (attending college, working for Home Depot, obtaining his welding license) and attacking the credibility of the two cooperators, Dinnerstein passionately wrapped up his summation:

> This case, ladies and gentlemen, is really about hope. My client, Anthony, he has hope to have a life, to get out of prison, to get a job, to return to his family, hopefully his welding license, he could get a job as a welder, hopefully he can get a job as an electrician.
>
> McQuilkin and Dowdie, they have hope too. Their hope is to try [to] figure out a way to get out from under the mess that they have created in their own lives. They will say anything, they will take down anyone, they will simply do anything to get out from under. That's what they have done their whole life, and that's what they are always going to do. As McQuilkin said, he said, I am selfish. That's right.
>
> Ladies and gentlemen, Anthony Praddy is not guilty of the most serious charges in these—in this indictment. He is not a participant in any sort of racketeering charges. He didn't commit a murder. He didn't possess a gun as part of this racketeering conspiracy. He knows nothing about the Raleigh Place Crew and whether or not it exists.
>
> The [fact] that the government says doesn't make it so. I ask you, ladies and gentlemen, to do justice here, to reach a verdict that speaks the truth, and as to those serious charges, not those four charges in the middle of the indictment, find him not guilty.

After Kiond Jones's lawyer tried his best to poke some holes in the government's damning case against his client, DuCharme, in rebuttal, wrapped up the summations, concluding that the jury should not convict the defendants because the government says they are guilty but "because the evidence proves they are guilty."

It was time for me to charge the jurors. It took a considerable amount of time for me to explain the law to them and how they should go about their deliberations, especially the need for a unanimous verdict on each count against each defendant. After three weeks of sitting silently while the trial unfolded, they then retired to the jury room to begin their deliberations. The fate of the defendants was now in their hands.

After deliberating for a few days, the jury returned its verdicts. It found the defendants guilty on all charges except two—the murder counts against Praddy.

Jones seemed to have an air of resignation as he was led back to jail, but even though Praddy had just been convicted of racketeering, racketeering conspiracy, four separate counts of marijuana distribution, marijuana distribution conspiracy, and the unlawful use of a firearm in connection with the drug conspiracy, he acted as if he had won and asked whether he could go home. When I told him I couldn't let him out of jail because he had just been convicted of a host of serious crimes that carry significant jail time, he seemed surprised.

Moreover, the government—as was its right—announced that it would retry him for the murder of Kevon Simon.

As is my custom after every trial, I make myself available to the jurors in the jury room. Many of my colleagues do this. It gives the jurors an opportunity to ask questions about whatever is on their mind. And it gives me an opportunity to explain to them how the judges run their chambers and handle their caseloads. The jurors appreciate the opportunity to "talk to the judge," especially after a multiweek trial. It's good PR for the judicial system. But I do not pry into their deliberations, and I never answer the one question they always ask: "Did we make the right decision?" I tell them that it is up to them, not the judge, to determine whether a defendant is guilty or not, and unless there was no view of the evidence at all to support a guilty verdict—which was clearly not the case here—no judge could set it aside.

But on this occasion I could sense some tension. As I scanned the room and listened to some of the jurors talk, it was clear that they really went head-to-head over whether Praddy shot Simon. I cautioned them not to discuss it with me, but from gratuitous comments that nonetheless were made, I sensed that most of the jurors were ready to convict Praddy of murder. He was that close to being sentenced to life.

The retrial took place the following April. It was significantly shorter than the first trial since there were no codefendants and there were only two counts that remained: whether Praddy was guilty of murder in aid of racketeering and the unlawful use of a firearm in connection with the murder—which obviously would automatically follow if Praddy was guilty of the murder charge. The retrial was basically a do-over. McQuilkin and Dowdie testified again, as did several of the collateral witnesses—such as the coroner who conducted the autopsy—and Detective Fonrose.

The government, however, had in the interim found another cooperator, who gave important testimony. Just before the trial, Andre Thomas was arrested on drug charges. He confessed to being a member of the Raleigh Place Crew and testified that a few days after Simon was killed, he saw Praddy with a gun. Nonetheless, even though the murder case was now even stronger than before, there was one major difference. It was a different jury.

This time the jurors were not hung on the murder counts. On May 2, 2011, Praddy was acquitted of killing Kevon Simon. I have no idea why. Did they believe that it was not intentional? Did they simply discredit the testimony of the cooperators? Did they believe Praddy's testimony? I didn't ask them, and they didn't tell me.

I immediately thought about the *Fitch* case and surmised that at Praddy's sentencing, the government would ask that I hold him accountable for murdering Kevon Simon. I was right.

The Punishment

In addition to Praddy, I also had to sentence Jones, Whyte, Thomas, and Dowdie. My colleague, Judge Vitaliano, had to sentence McQuilkin since he had handled his indictment; it sometimes randomly happens that not all cooperators are sentenced by the judge before whom they testified. I learned that Judge Vitaliano sentenced McQuilkin to "time served." He had been in jail for about a year before he became a cooperator and had been released five years ago. DuCharme told Judge Vitaliano that McQuilkin, who was then forty-eight, "has demonstrated extraordinary diligence, responsibility, and maturity in meeting his obligations under the cooperation agreement, and also just in conducting himself as a responsible adult member of the community." The probation department recommended that I sentence Jones to life—the maximum that Congress had established for the crimes of which he was convicted. I could have followed the recommendation: Although he was not charged with murdering anyone, he was an armed leader of the violent Raleigh Place Crew; he had attempted to murder someone and had participated in the kidnapping of another person. He had few redeeming qualities, having been arrested at least eleven times, with four prior convictions for an assortment of crimes. He was then thirty years old.

I gave him fifty years. If he behaved himself in jail, he could get 15 percent credit for good time and be released when he was seventy-two years old. If his health held out, he would not have to die in jail. I balanced this humane factor with the need to protect the public from this violent person.

I sentenced "Terror" Whyte to 135 months—a little more than eleven years. This was the recommendation of the probation department, and although I do not always follow its recommendations, I thought it was appropriate in this case. By pleading guilty to serious drug crimes, he had spared the government of the need to try him and deserved some credit for his acceptance of responsibility. He was then twenty-three and would be back on the streets in his early thirties.

I didn't put Thomas in jail. Because he had only pleaded to conspiring to sell marijuana and had fully cooperated with the government, I thought he deserved a break and that five years of probation was the right sentence.

If it were not for cooperators, there would be many more criminals walking the streets. As the government invariably points out when summing up to the jury—and did so again here—criminals usually don't hang out with model citizens, and it often takes a smaller criminal fish to catch and convict a bigger one. Cooperation agreements are such an important tool for the government that recent statistics reveal that 12 percent of all sentences were based on cooperation deals; in the EDNY—the home of many mafiosi and lots of gangs—it was even higher, at 22 percent. My colleague Judge Glasser had sentenced Salvatore "Sammy the Bull" Gravano to only five years—even though he confessed to killing lots of people—for ratting out the Teflon Don, John Gotti. It broke omertà and crippled the back of the Mafia.

I also cut Dowdie a big break. He had been in jail for a little more than two years, and I sentenced him to time served, even though he had pleaded guilty—as part of his cooperation deal—to kidnapping Hecclewood, conspiring to distribute a huge quantity of marijuana as the leader of the Raleigh Place Crew, and carrying a firearm in connection with his drug activities. This was about two years less than the probation department's recommendation, but I was impressed with the extent of his cooperation and the forthright manner in which he testified. Moreover, the government never would have known of all Dowdie's crimes if he chose to accept deportation instead of confessing to them and running a huge risk of spending the rest of his life behind bars.

But because of all the uncharged crimes Dowdie fessed up to, his advisory guidelines range was thirty years to life. They included participating with Jones in attempting to murder Hecclewood, another attempted murder, and another kidnapping. Upon reflection, I think I was too lenient on him—notwithstanding his profound cooperation—and probably should have given him a considerable amount of additional jail time. I felt somewhat better, however, when I recently ran into DuCharme, who told me that Dowdie, who was now almost fifty years old, has not had any other brushes with the law since I released him more than two years ago.

Praddy's sentence was a horse of a different color.

My decision in the *Fitch* case had been handed down just a few months before, and I started the sentencing proceeding by acknowledging that under the law, the judge—not the jury—has the responsibility to take into consideration, in fixing the sentence, uncharged conduct (as in *Fitch*) and even acquitted conduct, as in Praddy's case. This was now the moment when I had to decide whether to hold an acquitted defendant responsible for murder.

The government argued that the evidence clearly justified finding that Praddy killed Simon, and the probation department's presentence report recommended that—notwithstanding the jury's acquittal—I make the requisite murder finding and sentence Praddy to 420 months (thirty-five years). Under the law, five years was mandatory because of the conviction for carrying a gun. The other thirty years was the maximum that Congress had created for the drug crimes, which gave me—just like Judge Mahan in *Fitch*—enormous sentencing discretion.

I decided not to hold Praddy responsible for the murder of Kevon Simon. It was not an easy decision. As I commented: "I'm terribly concerned that there's a dead boy here and . . . there's a lot about what I heard that makes me suspect that maybe Mr. Dinnerstein's client was the killer."

And there were enough facts that I could find to support that conclusion. DuCharme had convincingly argued that the three cooperators were believable because they were picked up on separate occasions over a number of years and there was nothing to suggest that they had spoken to each other and coordinated their stories or that the government had put words into their mouths. I thought they were credible and did not lie on the witness stand.

On the other hand, I did not believe Praddy was testifying truthfully. He denied having twenty-seven bags of marijuana in his knapsack, even though he was caught red-handed by Detective Fonrose with those drugs—which were placed in evidence. And no one in their right mind would believe that Praddy had just bought the loaded gun that day, had never possessed a gun before, and didn't know why he bought it.

I remember the first time someone lied to me. It happened to be my mother. I think I was about three, and I could not tell the time yet. My mother had a routine that she followed each night before I had to go to bed. She would put on the radio and let me listen to The Lone Ranger—*it was my favorite serial radio show. It wanted to go to bed at 8 o'clock, like my friend Sherry Shapiro said he did, and my mother told me that* The Lone Ranger *played every night from 7:30 to 8:00. Of course I believed her. But when I finally figured out how to tell the time some months later, I learned that* The Lone Ranger *ended at 7 o'clock; my mother had tricked me into going to bed an hour earlier than I had thought. I had a hard time believing her after that and would get upset whenever I caught someone lying to me.*

My mother came from Fiddler on the Roof *country and told me stories about how the Cossacks would terrorize her little village. She was an overly protective mother and—given her upbringing—I came to understand why. She was a good, caring, stay-at-home mom. But she instilled some fears in me. To this day I am afraid of the water. I can't swim.*

She also had a love for music and always played the piano. She wasn't very good, but I caught the piano bug from her and music would become a big part of my life. I learned how to play boogie-woogie when I was nine, and playing jazz and writing songs would became my lifelong hobby.

My father was a good guy. And never once did he ever lie to me. His mother died giving birth to him. He manufactured cheap men's clothing with his cousins and made a good living. He was conservative. He would sit at home in a white shirt and tie. One day my oldest brother Leonard gave him a Humpty Dumpty paint-by-number set for my dad's new granddaughter. He did a perfect job following the dots. We gave him oils for his sixty-first birthday. I was in my last year of law school. He painted three beautiful landscapes during the next several months. We never knew he could do that. He was preoccupied with his business. He died eight months later. I promised myself that I would not let the law consume me. I would try to find out the full reach of whatever creative talents I might have before it was too late. I would try to be well rounded.

Since the *Praddy* case essentially was all about credibility, I reasoned that "it's not the same as if you have absolute . . . evidence that I can latch on to other than having to rely upon credibility." In my mind, this was the big difference between *Fitch* and this case. Added to the mix was my intuitive discomfort with countermanding a jury's verdict—even though under the law I could have, in effect, done that as a relevant sentencing factor for the racketeering and drug crimes of which the jury did convict Praddy.

But I still had to pick the number of years he would go to jail for those crimes. Here's where things really got heated. The requisite guidelines calculation came to a range of seventy-eight to ninety-seven months. Since the guidelines were now only advisory, I had the discretion to sentence Praddy to an out-of-guidelines sentence after carefully balancing the nature of the crimes and Praddy's personal characteristics. In most of my sentences, I have gone below the guidelines, but here I thought that an above-guidelines sentence was warranted because of Praddy's lies and the fact that the gun was loaded and the drug conspiracy was extensive. Praddy had admitted that he started to sell drugs in 2003 and was still selling just before he was arrested in 2009. And even though he started out when he was just a young kid, "what struck me [was] that after the murder, the unsolved murder of Kevon Simon, he continued selling drugs."

As expected, Dinnerstein did not take kindly to my thoughts:

> **DINNERSTEIN:** . . . [T]he government assumes that this is an evil kid and there isn't a way of convincing them different. That's the nature of this business. They're convinced he's evil. And the Court, though, has a harder job. It really does. It has the hardest job because your job is to paint a human face on this kid and not just to say he's an armed drug dealer; he's a murderer just like the government says. Your job is to try—and

it's damn hard, to figure out what's the right thing to do. Who is he? Who is he?

THE COURT: All right. We know we're going to have an unsolved murder here.

DINNERSTEIN: Well, that's true. Because they decided they were going to go after Anthony.

THE COURT: The result so far is that there is an unsolved murder. There's a boy who is dead.

DINNERSTEIN: Sure, it would have been nice if in 2004—

THE COURT: It means the . . . file is going to be closed as an unsolved murder.

DINNERSTEIN: That's terrible, too. And in 2004, if they had done a proper investigation, maybe they would have solved it.

THE COURT: Anything else?

DINNERSTEIN: I guess I wish I thought you were listening to me a little bit, Judge, because I think you—

THE COURT: Watch out. Don't cross the line.

DINNERSTEIN: I'm not crossing any lines.

THE COURT: It may well be that your client is getting away with murder.

DINNERSTEIN: No, he's not, Judge.

THE COURT: It may well be. You don't know to the contrary. Next.

DINNERSTEIN: Well, I guess I'm just going back to: He's not evil. I wish you would look at him as not being evil and I hope you don't have the presumption that he's an evil person. He has a great family. He's tried to do good things with his life. He went through—I went through all those, that sort of stuff. This is not a résumé of a killer and I go back to just what Judy Praddy says at the beginning and what she told me. Be wise, Judge.

Dinnerstein was exhausted. As he stared at me with plaintive eyes, he told me that Anthony Praddy wanted to be heard—as was his right—before sentence was imposed. He had now been in jail for more than a year since his conviction, and, standing five feet away from me, with two marshals standing behind him, he timidly started out by saying that he would "like to apologize to the Court." I did not understand what he was apologizing for, but I imagine it was his way of trying to be contrite.

Praddy then thanked his family "for supporting me," and asked me to impose "a lenient sentence because in the future I want to live my life." He then paused, took a deep breath, and ended by blurting out: "I don't want to spend the rest of my life in jail. Thank you."

It was pretty dramatic stuff. I could have ended it there and pronounce my sentence, but something within me drove me to interact with him.

THE COURT: You know, if the jury had found you guilty, you would be spending the rest of your life in jail? That would have been the absolute sentence I would have had to impose on you under the law.

PRADDY: Yes.

THE COURT: That's how close you came.

PRADDY: Um, I thank Mr. Dinnerstein for, um, defending me. I apologize to the Court, yourself, the prosecutors. And I'm nervous.

THE COURT: Well, you can take your time. I'm here to listen to you, as long as it takes.

After another pause, which seemed much longer than the last one, Praddy continued:

PRADDY: Um . . . I . . . I want, I want to build. I want to build my future, you know. I want to work. I don't want to spend the rest of my life in jail and the longer I stay in jail the harder—

THE COURT: Well, you're not going to spend the rest of your life in jail unless you die of a heart attack as a young man.

PRADDY: I feel like I'm having one now. You know, I want to work. I want to build a family. And the longer I stay in is—the harder when I come out you know. Job opportunities. I got my foot in the door already. You know, I had jobs in the past. I have a welder's license. I'm not a bad person. I made wrong mistakes in the past, wrong choices, associate with the wrong people at times, but I don't want that to determine who I am as a person and what to do in my future. I want to do positive things for myself.

There was another pause—even longer than the last one. He was pleading for his life, and I was riveted as he brought his plea to an end:

PRADDY: And . . . I don't want to make you mad. I think—I don't want to make you mad, you know. I didn't kill anybody. My lawyer told me to tell you that. I don't want to make you more mad when determining my sentence. So, I don't want to frustrate you. I don't know what you think, you know. I'm sorry.

THE COURT: Are you sure you bought a loaded gun on the day that you were arrested? You don't have to answer that question. Is there anything else you want to say?

PRADDY: Well, for . . . for the minimum. I want a future. I know I want to change my life. I want, under the minimum, the minimum you know. I want to live a life. I want to have a chance to live my life. To be back with my family.

THE COURT: You're going to have that chance because the jury didn't render a sentence, though I think the first jury was close to doing it, between you and me. That would have required me to sentence you to jail for the rest of your life. And you're going to have that chance because I'm not going to sentence you for the murder of Kevon Simon. So, you're going to have a chance to come out of jail.

I then sentenced Anthony Praddy to fifteen years—ten years for the racketeering and drug convictions, plus the mandatory five years for the gun conviction. He was shaking as the marshals took him back to jail; his parents—sitting in the front row—cried. Dinnerstein stood frozen, and I was exhausted as I staggered out of the courtroom.

But it was not the end.

Praddy appealed. All appeals from the EDNY—as well as from all the other district courts in New York and the district courts of Connecticut and Vermont—are heard by the judges of the Court of Appeals for the Second Circuit. Dinnerstein was appointed by the circuit court to represent him on the appeal. He argued that the sentence was excessive because "the court in fact imposed that sentence because it believed Praddy had killed Belize." As he wrote in his brief, "the court seized on the temporal span of the conspiracy and the amount of marijuana dispensed . . . in a thinly veiled attempt to impose a sentence appropriate for the killer the district court believed him to be."

The court rejected the argument because I had said on numerous occasions that I was not going to hold Praddy responsible for the murder. It agreed that I had calculated the advisory guideline range appropriately and that my finding that Praddy had perjured himself was warranted. It also agreed that my upward departure was warranted. And it held that there was ample evidence to support the jury's verdict, explaining that it "must affirm so long as the jury, drawing reasonable inferences from the evidence, may fairly and logically have concluded that the defendant was guilty beyond a reasonable doubt."

But to my surprise it threw out the firearm conviction and the five years that was mandated on that charge and sent the case back to me for resentencing. It explained that under the law, there was—unlike the other charges—a five-year statute of limitations on that offense.

Since Praddy was found with the gun in 2004 and not federally prosecuted for possessing it in connection with the drug conspiracy until the superseding indictment in 2010, the government could not prosecute him for that crime at that late date.

The statute of limitations issue was never raised at the trial by Dinnerstein, and I never thought about it. But under the law, if the statute of limitations was implicated, it could be raised at any time since it might be a jurisdictional issue; thus, it could be raised for the first time before the circuit court at the time of the appeal.

In remanding the case for resentencing, the circuit court instructed that the new sentence would be "de novo on the affirmed counts"—meaning that the entire prior sentence of ten years on those counts was vitiated, and I would have to start all over again. I knew that once again Dinnerstein and I would be going toe-to-toe. I didn't particularly relish the thought.

It didn't take long. Dinnerstein was more emotionally charged than ever. Praddy had now been in jail for more than four years, and his lawyer still passionately believed that he only sold a small quantity of drugs throughout the years, was not part of any criminal gang, only carried a gun on the one occasion when he was caught, and—of course—had nothing to do with the murder of Kevon Simon.

The government's position was that I should still sentence Praddy to fifteen years because even without the gun conviction the basic facts were still the same. I thought to myself that I would not do that because I would only have sentenced Praddy to ten years if not for the gun conviction. I then let Dinnerstein have the floor. He was obviously agitated, and to my dismay started to say some terrible things about me:

> **DINNERSTEIN:** You know, last night, Your Honor, I hardly slept at all because I was thinking how am I going to be able to talk to you? How am I going to be able to get you to see Anthony Praddy as who he is, which is, frankly, a great kid with a great family.

THE COURT: He lied before me.

DINNERSTEIN: No, he didn't.

THE COURT: Under oath. I so found and I explained it.

DINNERSTEIN: You can make . . . You're not God. You're a judge in a role and you have an enormous amount of power. But that doesn't make you right because you say so. And this is what I was afraid of last night when I couldn't sleep.

THE COURT: What else do you want to say?

DINNERSTEIN: I have a lot to say, Judge.

THE COURT: I will give you a reasonable amount of time but not forever.

DINNERSTEIN: What I was thinking about what I was going to say in this courtroom, I was thinking, "Am I dealing with a guy who is so sure of his own mind that no matter what I say to him isn't going to make a damn bit of difference?"

THE COURT: I can give him 180 months. Do not be so certain about how I am in my own mind. There's a legal basis on which I can give, as the government requests 180 months, so watch what you are saying to me. What else do you want to say? Don't attack my integrity as a judge.

DINNERSTEIN: I'm not attacking your integrity.

THE COURT: Don't tell me I'm [not] God. Don't tell me any of that nonsense. You're crossing the line. Behave yourself.

DINNERSTEIN: I am behaving myself.

THE COURT: What else do you want to say?

DINNERSTEIN: It is not conscionable, Your Honor, in my opinion, to give a person who sells marijuana, 5 or 6 pounds or even 100 kilograms, as part of some conspiracy anything like ten years or fifteen years in jail. It's just not right. For you to give that type of time, you would have to believe, Your Honor, but I wish you were listening to me, I really do.

THE COURT: You do not think I listen to you?

DINNERSTEIN: No. I think you're impatient and you look angry at me.

THE COURT: Let me be clear. Am I happy with you? No. Will it affect the judgment I am going to give him based upon my view of the law, my sense of responsibility as a judge? Absolutely not. Now, what else do you want to say? I will stand by my record of nineteen years.

It is not easy to listen to a lawyer tell you that you are not God and that you are not listening to him. I was tempted to hold him in contempt and cautioned him that he was skirting the line. But Dinnerstein could not control himself, and things got even worse. He once again harped on his belief that I was holding Praddy responsible for the murder—which Dinnerstein said he did not commit. I cautioned him that he could not ethically vouch for his client and that "[t]he only person that knows what happened is this person standing next to you." And he once again accused me of not listening to him, telling me that he was talking to "deaf ears."

He was getting closer by the moment to being held in contempt—something I never had done before. I cautioned him again and tried to get him to calm down:

THE COURT: Watch what you are saying again, Mr. Dinnerstein. Whenever you say you are talking to deaf ears, whenever you talk about that, I am telling you it does not register as the proper conduct that a lawyer should engage in.

DINNERSTEIN: I wish I knew judge—

THE COURT: Just calm yourself. We have had a pretty good, tolerant relationship over the years. Don't tell me you are talking on deaf ears. Do not tell me I have not considered this case. I have painstakingly considered this case for years. Do not talk like that because I may have to do something which I really do not want to do if you continue to do that.

I suspect that most of my colleagues would have held Dinnerstein in contempt right then and there. I didn't do it.

I remember when I was also close to being held in contempt. A few years before I got the nod for the judgeship, I tried a criminal case in the Nassau County Court before Judge Edward Baker. I was told he had the reputation for being a holy terror on defense lawyers and was an over-the-top government judge. And the case I had was one that he really hated. Several middle-aged men had been arrested for having sex with teenage boys. I represented one of the defendants, who was the last to be tried. The others had all been convicted and Judge Baker ultimately sentenced them to more than twenty years of jail. My client, who was a respected elected public official from Marietta, Ohio (I think he may have once been the mayor), was—in his other life, when he would come to New York—a member, as were the other defendants, of NAMBLA (National Man/Boy Love Association). I was up against it—the boy whom he was charged with molesting was just twelve years old.

But I did my best, as was my ethical responsibility, to give my client his day in court and put the prosecutor to the task of convincing the jury that he was guilty by the high criminal standard of proof beyond a reasonable doubt. And I got lucky while cross-examining the people's chief witness. He was fairly inarticulate and had a shaky memory about a bunch of things. I was having a field day with him when suddenly Judge Baker decided—out of the blue—to take a break. I was furious. He interrupted my cross-examination just while I was going for the kill. I snapped: "Judge, that's not fair. You cannot interrupt the cross-examination like this. You are giving the prosecutor a chance to talk to the witness away from the jury and resurrect his testimony. I object. You can't do that."

Not surprisingly, the good judge was furious and said that after the trial he would be considering holding me in contempt. I told him that I didn't mean any disrespect but my client's rights were being trampled on and I just lost it. I asked the judge to instruct the prosecutor not to talk to the witness during the break. He refused to do that. The jury heard it all.

After the break, the witness took the stand again and I tried to pick up where I had left off. But I first asked him whether the prosecutor had talked to him. He admitted that she did, but couldn't specifically remember what they spoke about.

The jury deliberated for a long time, but could not reach a unanimous verdict. I spoke afterward with one of the jurors, who told me that he and some of the others were offended by the judge's behavior and would not vote to convict even though the defendant was probably guilty.

Although the government could retry my client, it let him plead to a misdemeanor and be sentenced to thirty days in the county jail. Considering that his codefendants would be spending decades behind bars, it was a huge victory. I imagine the government must have felt sheepish about what had happened, as I suspect Judge Baker did as well. Even though he had every right to do so, he did not hold me in contempt of court.

Dinnerstein started to get control of himself, and I let him continue to talk for a considerable amount of time. He basically was repeating everything he had said before at the last sentencing hearing, and I told him that what I really wanted to know was how his client had been behaving in jail. Under the law, rehabilitation is one of the factors that a judge can consider in rendering a sentence, and after reviewing the presentence report and listening to Dinnerstein's comments, I made the following comment:

> **THE COURT:** Well, he has the fortune of being represented with the skill of counsel, okay, and he gets the benefit of that

and he has been able to prove to the Court that he has been a model citizen while he has been in jail, that he has engaged in significant rehabilitation, he has a supportive family that is here, and even though I am not 100 percent thrilled with Mr. Dinnerstein's performance through all of the heated comments we have had to engage in today, still as a judge responsible for rendering a fair and just decision, I am going to give that some credibility. . . .

I then recounted the reasons why I gave Praddy ten years before I had tacked on the five years for the gun charge, and asked Praddy if he wished to speak before the new sentence was rendered. He did:

PRADDY: Good morning, Your Honor. How you doing? My name is Anthony Praddy.

THE COURT: I am not doing so well today because I do not like to have to sentence you. Okay.

PRADDY: I just want to thank my family for their continuous level of support and I thank Mr. Dinnerstein for his representation and also I just like for you to take a look at the things I have done while in custody as far as the drug programs, stop the violence, not receiving any infractions.

THE COURT: So it is good to hear that you have found some value to the opportunities that you were given while you were in jail, the drug problem, apparently other rehabilitation programs the Bureau of Prison has for people who are incarcerated. It's good for me to hear that, that they have been of value and that you took advantage of that and it was of some help to you apparently. You can tell me, you know, whether I am right or not. I'm glad to hear it.

PRADDY: You're absolutely right.

THE COURT: Education certificates, all of that. Sometimes from bad things positive things can happen, too. From the negative things, the most positive things can happen. There are times when people go to jail and they come out and they are worse off than they were before. I have had situations where people went to jail and they come out better because of it. Where you fall in that pendulum, I don't know, but it seems to me that, this may be strange to say this, that you have been able to take advantage of the opportunities that you have had even though your living has been restricted and just maybe in the totality of one person's life, this may prove to be beneficial even though you had to have your liberty curtailed. I don't know, it sounds like this may be a good example of where imprisonment has actually given somebody the opportunity to get their act together and maybe come out of jail a different and a better person than when he went to jail. You can correct me if you think I am not seeing this correctly, but having a real conversation between the judge and somebody who he has to sentence, I just want to let you know what goes on in my mind.

PRADDY: I agree a hundred percent with what you're saying. And also I just like to add the MTA job. I would like to take that job and I would like to return to my family and continue on this positive path in life. I understand the seriousness of the situation. I had time to reflect and, you know, I want to do something positive in my life. I don't want to waste my life. I'm not a kid. I'm getting older. I have to take care of myself. I have to provide for myself. The longer I stay in prison, the harder it's going to be for me when I get back out there. So, I'm just asking you to take a look at the letter that I wrote you, the recent letter, and with what the probation report says in paragraph 41, with my personal problems and everything I've done, all the certificates and Mr. Dinnerstein sent some memorandum. I'd like you to take that into consideration and I want to return to my family so I can be able to start my life.

I was impressed. Praddy was now twenty-six. He had spent the last four years behind bars, and he seemed to have made the best of a bad situation. He presented himself as a more mature, reflective person than when I last saw him years ago. I decided to reward him for his rehabilitation and cut his sentence by twenty-three months. As I explained:

> **THE COURT:** I could have easily sentenced you for 120 months for all the reasons that I sentenced you to 120 months before. Nothing has changed except you behaved well in jail and I do believe that you are really on the verge of rehabilitating yourself, and when you get out of jail in a couple of years, you're going to be a changed person and you will have a productive life with the continued support of your family. So, if I were a mean-spirited judge, I'd say, okay, knock off the five years. By the way, the law would allow me to sentence you for more than 120 months. Just want you to hear me clearly because I don't know what Mr. Dinnerstein tells you when I'm not here. The law allows me to sentence you to more than 120 months. Right? I don't think I would sentence you to 180 months. I probably could do that also. I could probably articulate a lot of reasons why I would continue that sentence, okay?
>
> Mr. DuCharme has given some reasons that the facts are the same; it is just the statute of limitations, but the underlying facts are the same if not for the statute of limitations. I am not going to do that. All right? But I could do that. And I could certainly sentence you to the 120 or 130 or 140 months, but I am not doing that, right?
>
> So I am going to keep everything I did before less the five years and I am going to knock off an additional twenty-three months, almost two years, because of how well you behaved in jail, because of the rehabilitation that you have shown in court after I sentenced you. It is a lot of time. So it paid to really behave yourself.
>
> I hope you behaved yourself not because you wanted to get your time cut down, but because you really have found value to your life by reason of the studies and everything you have done in jail. So it is going to be ninety-seven months, okay?

I then asked Dinnerstein if there was anything else he wished to say. He told me that Praddy's mother wanted to speak again; he also wanted to bury the hatchet between us and end the proceeding on a high note:

DINNERSTEIN: I asked the mother if she wanted to speak to you. I just want to say, Your Honor, that I actually have a great deal of respect for you. We may not necessarily—

THE COURT: You just lose it once in a while.

DINNERSTEIN: I probably do. But I do have a lot of respect for you and I think you do what you feel is right. We may disagree with that and that's the nature of the business.

THE COURT: All right. If his mother is here, if she wants to talk to me. I already gave the sentence out, but it's up to you.

Judy Praddy walked slowly to the bench from the back of the courtroom. She was elegantly dressed and spoke compellingly:

MS. PRADDY: Good afternoon. As you know, I represent my son Anthony. I thank Mr. Dinnerstein for representing him. I do appreciate your authority and your decision making. He is our son. We've missed him terribly. I know you've made your decision and I'm hoping you will still reconsider the decision that you've made because it seems like he's been gone from us a long time. We tell him we miss him. We're supporting him while he's where he is, but it's difficult not really having him in our presence. I know that Anthony, as Mr. Dinnerstein says, he's a good kid. He truly is a good kid. He's our son and I just hope that you would still—I appreciate what you've done and what you said in the decision that you made here today as the judge of this courtroom, however, I would still extend that you please reconsider even further. Give him the opportunity at this age to come out to civilization. I know, I know that he's going to be a positive contributor in society if he's given that opportunity again.

I didn't have to say anything, but I wanted to. I wasn't sure that she fully understood how close her son came to being in jail for the rest of his life. And I wanted to let her know that her son's assigned counsel was the big difference. While Dinnerstein admittedly "lost it" on a few occasions, he was a true believer in his client's innocence—except for the relatively minor four separate drug charges for which he was caught red-handed—and did everything in his power to give him the finest representation, equal, if not better, than the most celebrated criminal defense lawyers. While I came close to holding him in contempt—for good and sufficient reasons—I would not hesitate to assign him to the most difficult and challenging criminal cases in the future.

Judy Praddy listened respectfully as I spoke:

THE COURT: Well, I think the fact that you're speaking to me gives me some comfort that, you know, when he gets out of jail in a couple of years—it's not going to be twenty, it's not going to be life—that he will have the support of family and hopefully you will guide him in the right direction.

I am glad you came here and spoke this way, but I want you also to realize how, as I mentioned before, how fortunate he is. Look at the negatives and look at the positives also to try to balance out all of your emotionality. I just want you to realize you got, by luck of the draw, assigned a counsel free of charge because of the great system of justice in the United States of America unlike other countries in the world. Right? And you are not going to find a finer lawyer, you know, and a more passionate lawyer than Mr. Dinnerstein. That's luck, I guess.

We would like to think that all of the lawyers that we assign to represent people who cannot afford a lawyer are equally competent, but in the real world, that is not the way it works out. Just like not all judges are the same, not all lawyers are the same, right? So number one, I just want you to really realize that.

Number two, what I want you to also realize, because I know that you are emotional obviously as a mother just to look at this in maybe one perspective. I am trying to give you a broader perspective while we are talking in open court today, which I think is a healthy thing for the system of justice to do. It shouldn't be the routine kind of judge coming out here and saying here's what happens. So we have a meaningful discussion, right?

As I mentioned before, a less skilled lawyer who is not arguing as passionately as Mr. Dinnerstein—the [first] jury didn't acquit him of murder. They just couldn't come to a unanimous agreement. All right? I don't know what the jury count was. It may have been eleven to one for conviction, for all I know. I don't know. All right. But . . . maybe the same jurors could have sent your son to jail for life and the judge would not have been able to overturn that decision in all probability. All right? So that's the second thing you should be very grateful of.

The third thing you should be grateful of is that notwithstanding the fact that I have been very critical of Mr. Dinnerstein and some of the comments he made impugning my professional integrity and I got a little bit hot under the collar because I, too, am a human being, right, notwithstanding that, I didn't hold that against him. I could have done that if I was a mean-spirited person. And I gave him credit for the fact that he had behaved himself well in jail and he seems to be going in the right direction and I'm comforted by the fact that he has the support of his family that will keep that motivation going and that he will come out and be a productive member of society. So, you have a lot that—if you can balance this thing emotionally, you may not be able to do that—you should be very thankful for, even though the sentencing is something that you prefer did not happen.

So if he gets credit, he'll get credit for 15 percent for being well behaved in jail. I mean, obviously, that is what is going to happen here because he had done a great job. So knock off 15 percent from ninety-seven months. You can do the math. He gets credit for four years in jail. He is going to be out in a couple of years.

I hope I do not have to see him here again. He is going to be under supervision for five years, so we are going to see how he adjusts to society because if he violates any of the conditions of supervised release, obviously there are going to be big problems.

You are going to have a big responsibility to make sure that his supervision and his rehabilitation is going to be perfect.

MS. PRADDY: We're ready to take on that responsibility today.

THE COURT: Right. So we get glowing reports from the probation department because I am going to really keep a watch on that.

MS. PRADDY: I mean today, releasing him today, we're willing to take on that responsibility.

THE COURT: We're not going to release him today.

MS. PRADDY: But it's not just me. It's his family.

THE COURT: I understand that. I understand all of that, but I have spoken about all I can say, all I am going to say. If there is nothing else, I thank you for coming, and keep up the good work. All right? So I think this concludes the resentencing. Thank you.

To this day, it's hard for me to get the Praddy case out of my mind. I often think that as much as we hope to achieve justice, we know that guilty people are on the streets and innocent folks are in jail. I believe that our country does a better job than others to get it right, but given that human beings—with all their frailties—are passing judgment on others, it's bound to happen.

Did the second jury get it right when it acquitted Praddy? As I told Dinnerstein, I had my doubts. But I wondered whether Dinnerstein was right when he told the appellate court that I sentenced Praddy more harshly because I truly believed that he killed Kevon Simon. I tried not to do that but I can't speak for my subconscious. I just didn't think Praddy was the angel that Dinnerstein thought he was. And there was no doubt in my mind that Praddy outright lied under oath when he testified. That bothered me a lot. But I still wonder whether subconsciously I believed that Praddy killed Simon, and that—not-

withstanding my denials—it might have been the major factor in upwardly departing from the guidelines range?

~

In the end, there remains an unsolved capital crime. Maybe Dowdie, McQuilkin, Jones, or Thomas was the real killer. Or maybe it was cousin Lindsey—whose whereabouts have always been unknown—or another member of the Raleigh Place Crew. Or just maybe the government got it right and Anthony Praddy got away with murder. I guess we'll never know for sure, but it was time to move on.

3

Victim Impact Testimony

The Carreto Family

The Crime

There was no guessing this time. Consuelo Carreto Valencia's two sons—plus a few others—pleaded guilty, rather than face almost certain conviction by a jury, for luring vulnerable young Mexican girls into the United States and forcing them into prostitution as sex slaves.

The indictment, containing twenty-seven counts, was handed down on November 16, 2004. In addition to Consuelo Carreto's sons—Josue and Gerardo—it also named her and three others as codefendants, Daniel Perez Alonso, Eliu Carreto Fernandez, and Maria De Los Angeles Velasquez Reyes.

Daniel was Josue's friend, Eliu was Josue and Gerardo's first cousin, and Maria was the widow of Josue and Gerardo's deceased brother, Israel, who had been kidnapped and killed in Mexico a few years before. All the defendants were charged in each count.

The overarching charge was that they all conspired with each other and with others to smuggle young Mexican women into the United

States, transport them to New York City, compel them "through physical violence, sexual assault, threats of harm, deception, false promises, and coercion to engage in prostitution at various brothels," and require them to turn over all their illicit proceeds to the defendants.

The indictment named nine "Jane Does" as victims. They were each young Mexican girls; one was only fifteen. In addition to the conspiracy charge, the indictment was broken down into three substantive sets of related crimes committed against each of these victims by each of the defendants: sex trafficking; forced labor, and Mann Act violations—all dealing with various criminal aspects associated with bringing the victims into the country for purposes of prostitution.

The Carreto case was trumpeted by the U.S. Attorney's Office as the leading case in the country to bring the full force of the law down upon sex traffickers. I didn't realize the extent or magnitude of this abhorrent criminal activity until then, and I am struck to this day about how rampant it has become. In the State Department's June 2014 *Trafficking in Persons Report*, Secretary of State Kerry estimated that in the world today there are "more than 20 million victims of trafficking," and there is "perhaps no greater assault on basic freedom than the evil of human trafficking."

The government believed that its case was overwhelming. There was little doubt that Congress viewed the crimes as among the most serious; if they were convicted, I could sentence the defendants to life. The government gave me the following overview of their alleged criminal misdeeds:

> The Carreto family, whose members and associates lived in or around Tenancingo, Mexico, operated an extensive sex trafficking ring, wherein young women and girls were compelled to perform acts of prostitution for paying customers. They used force, fraud, and coercion to control the victims and thereby ensure that they would engage in prostitution. Specifically, the Carreto family recruited numerous young women into prostitution in Mexico prior to bringing them to New York. In some instances, members or associates of the Carreto family immediately raped or beat the victims in Mexico, breaking them down

and overcoming their wills quickly. Other times, they engaged in a courtship with the victims in Mexico with false promises of marriage and a better life. These false promises ultimately led to the use of isolation, coercion, and fraud to compel the victims into prostitution. The victims were completely isolated from family and friends, forbidden to go out alone; required to give virtually every cent that they received from prostituting themselves to members or associates of the Carreto family; and severely beaten if they refused to engage in prostitution, hid money, came home late, contacted their families on their own, or disobeyed orders.

Although the indictment named six defendants, two of them had yet to be arrested and taken into custody. Consuelo Carreto and her daughter-in-law Maria were believed to be in Mexico, and efforts were under way to find them and have them extradited. The others—Josue, Gerardo, Daniel, and Eliu—were picked up in New York and would have to stand trial before me.

In addition, the government had separately indicted Eloy Carreto Reyes—a nephew of the Carreto brothers—for forcing his wife to become a prostitute. He pleaded guilty to that charge before me, and I would have to sentence him at a later date. The government also separately indicted Edith Mosquera de Flores for running a brothel in Brooklyn where the victims serviced her customers. The madam had pleaded guilty before me to operating the brothel and confessed to chauffeuring the victims to her den of iniquity in her minivan and keeping half the money earned by them. I would also have to eventually sentence her.

Moreover, Eliu had worked out a separate plea deal, and on December 22, 2004, the government allowed him to plead guilty before a magistrate judge to one of the twenty-seven counts—charging him with forcing one of the nine victims to become a prostitute. The other charges were dropped, and he—in addition to Eloy and the madam—would also have to be sentenced by me.

As for the Carreto brothers and their friend Daniel, the government had extended a global plea offer to them, which meant that they all had to agree to it, and on February 17, 2005, I had these defendants, their lawyers, and the government's lawyer appear before me to find out what was happening. Josue and Gerard had each retained their own lawyers—Ted Del Valle and Michael Musa-Obregon, respectively; Daniel Perez Alonso could not afford one, so I appointed a CJA lawyer—Alan Lashley—to represent him. The government was represented by Daniel Alonso, who quickly assured me that he was not related to his namesake.

Under the federal law, the judge is not permitted to engage in plea negotiations, but the government disclosed that under the proposed plea deal, the defendants would be allowed to plead to four of the twenty-seven counts—one conspiracy count and three of the nine sex-trafficking victim counts. I advised the defendants that if they accepted the offer, they would not have to go to trial on the other twenty-three counts, which would be dismissed. I had to carefully advise them that I could not tell them what their sentences would be at that time and that they obviously might be facing serious jail time. But certainly they would not have to run the risk of being convicted of all twenty-seven counts, and their sentences would undoubtedly be less.

The lawyers told me that the government had made a "reverse proffer," meaning that it laid bare all the evidence that it would present at trial. After assessing it, the lawyers, as was their professional obligation, gave their clients their best advice. They recommended that they accept the plea offer.

The Carreto brothers were willing to do it, but not Daniel. He said he was not guilty of sex trafficking and was only willing to plead guilty "for having entered the country illegally." Since there would be no global plea, the government then revoked its plea offer. It had the right to do that. It sounds like blackmail, but the government did not have to offer the plea deal in the first place. Global pleas are not uncommon. The government is willing to do it to save the time and expense of going through a protracted trial, even if it has an airtight case; and, of course, there can never be a guarantee of what a jury might do.

It is imperative that the defendants understand the consequences of turning down a plea offer, and it is the judge's responsibility to make sure that they do. This is especially important where—as here—Daniel complained about his lawyer; I had denied a previous request that I replace Mr. Lashley with a new CJA lawyer. I carefully tried to do that:

> THE COURT: Mr. Perez, I have heard three lawyers talk about how painstakingly they read the plea agreement, explained the law to you, they explained the law of conspiracy, they explained the law of sex trafficking. You understand all of that. And they did explain all of this to you thoroughly; yes or no?
>
> DANIEL: Yes. Only I came here with my wife and my couple [sic] and nothing else.
>
> THE COURT: Well, I understand that. Okay. That's your position. And Mr. Lashley has worked hard also to explain everything to you, as well? Yes or no?
>
> DANIEL: Some part of it, no, he didn't.
>
> THE COURT: But now you understand everything; correct?
>
> DANIEL: Yes.
>
> THE COURT: And Mr. Lashley was there working with you this morning with the other lawyers to explain everything to you?
>
> DANIEL: He only read to me the agreement and the conspiracy.
>
> THE COURT: And the other lawyers explained things to you, too; right?
>
> DANIEL: Yes.
>
> THE COURT: Is there anything at all about what was said to you that you don't understand by Mr. Lashley, by Mr. Musa-Obregon, by Mr. Del Valle? Anything at all?

DANIEL: No, everything is okay.

THE COURT: Okay. Let's go forward.

ALONSO (the government's lawyer): I guess the question I was looking for is that if he's convicted down the road and he gets a sentence more severe than what's in the plea agreement, that he can't complain that anyone did anything wrong.

THE COURT: Just understand that. I mean, I am clear about that in my mind that if the matter goes forward and you get convicted, and you're sentenced to a term of incarceration which is greater than possibly might have been the case under the plea agreement, you cannot come back and say Mr. Lashley did not explain everything to me in respect to the plea agreement or I did not understand what the consequences were of pleading guilty or not guilty pursuant to the plea agreement. You [have] assured me in court today that you understand everything. I am just letting you know that that is my understanding. Do you agree with that or not?

DANIEL: Yes.

THE COURT: Let's go forward. We have no choice here but to go forward with the trial.

Before I set the trial date, the other defendants chimed in. Josue "ask[ed] forgiveness for having invaded your country" and said he would only plead guilty "as to what I did"—which apparently did not include sex trafficking. And Gerardo asked for the appointment of new counsel because his lawyer had told him he wanted another $50,000 if the case went to trial; Mr. Obregon assured me that this was not the case. Not to be outdone, Daniel then also asked for a new attorney. I denied the eleventh-hour requests to change attorneys. The trial would start in six weeks.

Shortly after I graduated from Cornell, I met Estelle, who would become my first wife. She was—and still is—a smart, decent person, and we stayed married for many years, but there were tensions in the relationship, probably due in large part to my working too hard to handle the pressures of building a law practice from scratch. Nonetheless, we had many good times together, and two children. Our son, Neil, turned out to be a successful, well-liked, and highly regarded labor lawyer, and our daughter, Nancy, became a skilled and super-talented psychiatric social worker.

I thought about Nancy during the Carreto case. I remember having successfully represented a defendant who was charged with rape and being confronted by a friend who could not understand how I could do that. Moreover, he asked me what I would have done if my client had raped my daughter. I snapped back: "I would probably kill him." But I also told him that I could easily separate my emotions from my responsibility as a lawyer to make sure that I could give my client the best representation I was capable of, which—just as in the NAMBLA case—I did. When I became a judge, I realized how important it would be to check out whatever emotional baggage I might possibly have in any given case and try to apply the law in a fair, even-handed, and objective manner, although I recognized that it might be easier said than done.

The jury was selected on April 4, 2005. The next morning, just before the jurors were to be brought into the courtroom and the trial was to begin, the government's lawyer—the good Alonso—announced that the defendants' lawyers had told him that their clients didn't want to go forward with the trial and would plead guilty to the entire twenty-seven-count indictment. I was stunned. This never had happened before—and has never happened since. While I have had a few defendants who got religion a few days before their trial was to start, nothing before ever came close to this—pleading to a huge multicount indictment moments after the jury had been selected and the trial was about to begin.

It was important for me to find out what caused this collective change of heart, especially since the government had estimated that the range of imprisonment under the advisory guidelines for the twenty-seven crimes was a whopping 324 to 405 months for both Carretos, and 292 to 365 months for Daniel. So I asked each lawyer, "[W]hy is it in your client's best interest to plea to the entire indictment in lieu of going to trial? It seems to me, at least at a glance, that the punishment would likely be the same, be it by plea or be it by conviction; maybe there's something about that that I don't fully understand." Before they responded, the government's lawyer chimed in:

> **ALONSO:** You are the sentencing judge. There is an intangible value to two things. One is to throw themselves on your mercy because they believe after trial they will be convicted because they now know, after seeing the 3500 material, that the case is overwhelming against them, and so there is that intangible value. The guidelines, of course, are advisory. You will hear arguments, I'm sure, at sentencing that you should [sentence them] below the range that we set forth, and the range that you find—the range we set forth may not be the one you ultimately find. The second is that you are going to be seeing the evidence in the case through the cold reading of a presentence report, as opposed through live testimony of witnesses.

The "3500 material" that the government's lawyer referenced referred to all the statements of witnesses the government intended to call. It is required to disclose all such statements just prior to trial. Here, they obviously were the statements made to the government by the nine victims; they must have been devastating.

And Mr. Alonso was correct that the guidelines were now advisory—the Supreme Court had just recently come down with its decision in *Booker*—and I was no longer bound to sentence a defendant within the guidelines' range.

I then directed pointed questions to each lawyer to make sure that his client fully understood the risks he was taking. Each defendant would have to allocute to the crimes—meaning he would have to confess before me, in his own words, to each of the twenty-seven crimes. And there would be no guarantee as to what the sentence would be.

First I spoke to Josue's lawyer:

> **THE COURT:** You concur in Mr. Alonso's supposition that by obviating the need to have a three-week trial and to put all of these folks on the stand and to have all of the evidence formally introduced at trial, that perhaps the sentencing judge may look upon the dynamics more favorably when sentencing comes to pass, and that I would exercise my authority even in a more favorable way; is that basically your take on this?
>
> **DEL VALLE:** It is not only my take; it is my hope. I cannot pretend to predict the future, Your Honor, but it is certainly something I would look at.
>
> **THE COURT:** When we [go] through the allocution, I will tell your client—all of the clients—that I'm not giving them any promises or guarantees, and that the sentence might well be more strict than they would hope it would be. Are they prepared to go forward with that understanding?
>
> **DEL VALLE:** They are indeed, Your Honor. They understand that. In fact, when we reviewed the allocution with our clients, we indicated whatever estimates the government has in fact given, the final sentence rests on Your Honor. Your Honor is the only one who will decide what the sentence will be.

Next, I heard from Gerardo's attorney:

> **MUSA-OBREGON:** The government has spent a lot of time already preparing for trial, but I don't think all their resources have been expended. I know for the defendants to put the government in a position of flying so many witnesses in in terms of having each of the witnesses relive the experiences that our clients are accused of will inevitably have a worse impact on the court than the actual plea. There are elements of these crimes

that call for a life imprisonment–type sentence, but by my client pleading guilty to this, he helps his bets with respect to avoiding—potentially avoiding—a life sentence.

Last, I addressed Daniel's lawyer:

THE COURT: Mr. Lashley, last but not least, your client in particular expressed dissatisfaction with your representation. We spent a good deal of time discussing that at prior occasions. I'm not going to repeat what those discussions were all about. But I want to make my best efforts to make sure I will not have to deal with any collateral matters, if your client goes forward and pleads, in light of the fact that he's protested continuously about your legal representation, not to cast any aspersions against you. I'm just setting the record straight. So hopefully by having this colloquy this morning, it would make it less probable . . . I would have to deal with 2,255 collateral matters and have to process arguments that you didn't properly advise him, that he wasn't given effective counsel. I think it is important for us to engage in these prophylactic measures at this particular time. So I want to hear from you now, in light of the fact that your client has expressed displeasure in your representation in the past. Of course I will speak to him about that extensively, and in light of the fact that now, contrary to what he said on prior occasions, he is willing to plead to the entire indictment. It strikes me that we have to be very cautious about understanding exactly what has transpired in court. Maybe you can educate the court about that.

LASHLEY: Judge, I appreciate what you are doing. I think it is the right thing this morning. We had a status conference here last Thursday, if you recall, before the trial, and at that time everyone indicated they wanted to go to trial. Yesterday morning we came in here and picked the jury, and my client said he wanted to speak to me. He told me that he had changed his mind and does not want to go to trial and wants to plead to the indictment, because he knows the time expired for the plea agreement back in February. He told me that he feels that he went through the plea—I'm sorry, if he pled guilty today, he would have a possibility of not facing life in jail because there would be circumstances I can argue to the court at the time of sentencing. We now have the [Supreme Court] decisions where the guidelines are not mandatory; they are advisory. All of these things you can consider and hopefully [give] him a sentence lower than he would have gotten if he went to trial. I went through all of the questions with him and discussed everything with co-counsel, with the prosecutor, and I feel confident that he wants to plead guilty today.

What was unspoken was that the lawyers must have known of my reputation as a fairly lenient sentencer. Even before the guidelines became advisory, I had often departed below the ranges in the handful of cases where downward departures were authorized, such as for extreme emotional and physical problems and aberrant behavior, and I had never given an above-guidelines sentence. And now that the guidelines had been made advisory, I started to regularly issue sentences below the advisory guidelines range where I thought the range was too extreme and that the defendants had some positive personal characteristics.

The fallout from the Supreme Court's 2005 decision in *Booker* has been significant. The most recent sentencing statistics compiled by the U.S. Sentencing Commission—for the year 2017—reveal that, nationwide, 20.1 percent of all sentences were below the advisory guidelines range. In the EDNY it was much higher—44.7 percent. And I would estimate that more than half of my sentences were below the range. As for above-guidelines sentences, they were rare: 2.9 percent nationwide and 2.1 percent in the EDNY.

Knowing my reputation, I imagine the defendants' lawyers must have told their clients that it was improbable that I would give them an above-guidelines sentence. Nonetheless, before I listened to the defendants' allocutions, I made sure that they understood that I was not making any promises: Only after I received the presentence report and considered all of the arguments that the defendants' lawyers would be making at the sentencing proceeding—which would not take place for several months while the report was being prepared—could I arrive at the sentence.

I then listened to each defendant's allocution. Through a Spanish interpreter, they one by one read from a prepared statement. Josue Flores Carreto went first:

> **JOSUE FLORES CARRETO:** Veronica R., Veronica P., Virginia G., and Maria Del Rayo G., we smuggled them into the United States of America from Mexico, with intention of forcing them to engage in prostitution. The services that I forced Veronica R., Veronica P., Virginia G., and Maria Del Rayo were commercial sexual acts. They were coming to almost every day to different brothels in the counties of Brooklyn, Queens, in the city of New York. I knew that Veronica R. was under eighteen years old when she was first recruited. I forced those women to engage in commercial sexual acts through threats of causing them injury and physical restriction. I assaulted physically Veronica R., and she suffered physical injuries as a result of those assaults. I assaulted her physically for disobeying my orders in reference to prostitution jobs. I smuggled those women into New York from Mexico, so that they could engage in prostitution. I did not allow Veronica R. to keep any of the money that she received from engaging in prostitution. I kept some of the money and sent money to Mexico to the other participants in this illegal activity. I aided and abetted Gerardo Flores Carreto and Daniel Perez Alonso in their acts with Veronica R., Veronica P., Virginia G., and Maria Del Rayo. I acted knowingly in the commission of all of those acts. I was an organizer and one of the bosses in this criminal activity that involved five or more participants.

The named victims were Jane Does one through four of the indictment. While Josue made no mention of the other five victims in the indictment—Jane Does five through nine—he had pleaded guilty to each of the crimes contained in the indictment: sex trafficking, forced labor, smuggling, and violation of the Mann Act. The other defendants' allocutions were essentially the same, with slight variations. Gerardo added Olivia G. to the mix, who was also under eighteen, and Daniel said he was only a supervisor—rather than an organizer—of the criminal activity.

I elicited from the defendants that they were also each coconspirators in their criminal misdeeds and then ended the day's dramatic events:

> **THE COURT:** At this time the court makes the following determinations: That based on all of the information given to me in these lengthy proceedings today, I find that each defendant is acting voluntarily, fully understands his rights and the consequences of his pleas, and that there are indeed factual bases for each of the pleas. I, therefore, accept the pleas of guilty to each of these twenty-seven counts. You will be notified in due course, gentlemen, of the sentencing date. As I mentioned before, it is necessary for the probation office to prepare an elaborate presentence report which will have a lot to do with your sentencing. It takes some period of time for them to do that. It may take a few months. You would have the right to have counsel present with any meeting with the probation office. Many times they wish to meet with the defendants to ask questions and to give the defendants the opportunity to participate in the preparation of the report, and you have the right to [the] aid of counsel with respect to that, if you wish to avail yourself of that opportunity. I think that completes the proceedings.

The jurors had been waiting patiently in the jury room while all this was happening. I went into the room, told them what had happened, thanked them for their service, and sent them home. The marshals who had been assigned to guard against any possible disturbances in the courtroom took the defendants back to jail to await their fates.

The Punishment

I sentenced the madam, Edith Mosquera de Flores, to twenty-seven months for running her Brooklyn brothel and working with the Carreto brothers to facilitate their victims' prostitution. Moreover, she kept half of the victims' hard-earned monies. And they surely were hard-earned, often requiring the "servicing" of up to twenty of her customers each day, who paid the rather meager sum of $25 for the opportunity to violate them. I wondered who these people were. Edith Mosquera de Flores was then a dowdy-looking fifty-one-year-old woman who in her better-looking days had also been a prostitute. Perhaps that is why she was so callous toward the victims' plight.

I gave Eliu—who was then thirty-seven years old—eighty months for enslaving Jane Doe 4 and physically forcing her to be a prostitute, and I sentenced Eloy—who was then twenty-five—to "time served" for compelling his own wife to be a prostitute; he had been in jail for just about three years.

On April 27, 2006, the principal defendants—Gerardo, Josue, and Daniel—appeared before me to be sentenced. As was my practice, I gave their lawyers a copy of the probation department's Sentence Recommendations and its accompanying comments. Over the years I have found that its recommendations—though well intended and thoughtfully made—were usually on the high side and my sentences have generally been significantly—but not always—lower. The comments have invariably been right on and succinctly have gone right to the heart of the defendants' misdeeds. Here, the comments were the same for both Carreto brothers—their focus was on the plight of the victims:

> The victims in this case have suffered immensely. The defendants controlled every aspect of their lives; the women were searched for money as they were not allowed to keep any of that which they earned; some were required to service more than twenty customers a day, then beaten when they did not earn enough money and repeatedly threatened with death. In addition to the rapes, one victim was forced to have an abortion when she became pregnant as a result of a rape by one

of the defendants. The crimes against these women are horrific and inhumane. Further, the advisory guideline range, although high, does not take into consideration all of the victims in this case. The nature and seriousness of the offense, coupled with the aggravating factors of the number of victims not considered in the advisory guidelines as well as the history and characteristics of the defendant and the need for punishment and deterrence, call for a sentence of thirty-five years' custody.

The comments for Daniel were similar, but he was considered somewhat less culpable and the probation department's recommendation was twenty-five years.

The presentence report also contained written statements from each of the nine Jane Doe victims named in the indictment. They constituted "3500 material" that the government was obliged to turn over to the defendants prior to trial, and would have been the basis of the victims' trial testimony. They were devastating and I imagine were the main reason why the defendants decided to plead to the entire indictment and avoid listening to each of the victims tell the jury about their brutal mistreatment. While all of the Victim Impact Statements had the same basic tone, one particularly caught my eye:

Victim Impact Statement of Olivia G.

To the Judge: My name is Olivia G. . . . I am writing to you so that you know what Gerardo Flores Carreto and his family have done to me and the great harm they have caused me. The reasons for which are that to begin with he raped me; then he forced me to have an abortion, not allowing me to have it confirmed except that I knew because I had not menstruated and after he took me to a private clinic and I was given an injection and I got my period back. It was an abortion. Afterwards he forced me to do things that I did not want to do but I had to do them because I was far away from my family and I did not know what else to do, only what he said. What I never agreed on was that he set me up as a prostitute when I was fifteen years old and since that age my nightmare began with him. He used to beat me up, threaten me that I would not see my parents when he had promised my parents that I would visit them often, yet he did not keep that promise. After [I worked] as a prostitute, he would beat me up for not giving him or bringing him the money he demanded. After he got me pregnant he asked me if I wanted to have the baby or not. I told him I did, so then he answered that I would still have to work for four months of the pregnancy in order to have money to support her. He was always making promises that he never kept, like that I would only work as a prostitute for two years and it turned out to be much longer. He told me that when we had a child I was not going to continue working and it did not turn out that way; instead after four months of pregnancy I continued working. After I had the baby girl his mother, Consuelo Carreto, came at me and told me not to become very fond of the baby because the baby would become used to me and I had to get back to work. At that time Gerardo Flores Carreto told me that if I did not continue doing the same kind of work he would steal my daughter from me.

And I want him to stay in jail for the maximum time allowed by the law.

Before the sentencing proceeding got under way, the defendants' lawyers said that their clients wanted to withdraw their guilty pleas. It did not sit well with me. I had carefully explained at the plea proceedings that I would not allow them to do that. Moreover, I painstakingly had made sure that they understood the consequences of their pleas, that they really wanted to plead guilty to the entire indictment, and that they were satisfied with their lawyers. But they persisted, and their lawyers gave me a Spanish document from some alleged investigator the defendants had hired that purportedly contained some statements by a few of the victims—when they and the defendants were in Mexico some time ago.

As Gerardo's lawyer, Mr. Musa-Obregon, explained:

Your Honor, on behalf of Gerardo Carreto Flores. This morning upon arriving in court, I met with an investigator that was hired by all three defendants collectively. That investigator is a gentleman by the name of Willie Acosta. Mr. Acosta was working for the defendants without the supervision of counsel and he went to Mexico over the last month.

He had contacted all three of the defense lawyers and indicated to us previously that there existed some transcripts from a proceeding in Mexico that contained exculpatory information with respect to the statements that were made by three of the victims in the proceedings here that were also taken in Mexico.

All three counsel urged the investigator that if these transcripts indeed existed to bring them to our attention and bring them to us immediately.

Last night I received a call at about 10:30 at night from the investigator where he called me generically, but did not mention that these transcripts existed until I directly asked him, "Well, do you have these transcripts?" He said, "Yes."

I then made arrangements for him to bring them to court this morning. Upon my arriving, I perused the transcripts and they do appear to have sworn statements of fact by three of the victims in this case where they directly contradict their position before the government—

I made short shrift of this last-minute ploy to avoid judgment day by simply rhetorically asking: "So if they had all this information and they knew what happened in Mexico, why pray tell did they plead guilty?" Needless to say, these shenanigans did not sit well with me, and we proceeded with the sentencing. I first dealt with the Carreto brothers and calculated the advisory guideline range for each of them to be 360 to life.

Gerardo's lawyer made a pitch for a lenient sentence because he believed that his client's behavior was "to some extent a product of his environment," explaining that "in the town where he is from, prostitution is something that occurs very frequently. Many households, many families are involved in prostitution." I asked Mr. Musa-Obregon whether it might be appropriate to "perhaps send a message to others who may want to come to the United States because they think prostitution is A-okay and everything also that happened here is okay?" The colloquy between us continued:

> THE COURT: You don't think they should be dealt harshly and a message should be sent that this is not going to be accepted in this country? Especially since you tell me it's okay in Mexico.
>
> MUSA-OBREGON: Judge, I'm not saying it's okay. I'm saying it happens in that particular town.
>
> THE COURT: Maybe it won't happen in this country if the proper message is given. Go ahead.
>
> MUSA-OBREGON: Your Honor, I think Mr. Carreto—
>
> THE COURT: We are not in Mexico. I love Mexico. Don't get me wrong; we have different laws and different concepts of justice, perhaps.
>
> MUSA-OBREGON: Your Honor, I think in this particular case, Mr. Carreto should be judged and sentenced according to his own actions. And I don't think this should be a test case or anything of the sort where I know the government spent millions of dollars on this particular case—
>
> THE COURT: I'm going to sentence somebody because they pled guilty to twenty-seven terrible counts of criminal behavior. That's why I'm going to sentence him. And it's going to be based upon the facts that I have and the law that I'm going to apply. That's all I'm going to do. Nothing else.

Gerardo's lawyer asked me "to consider sentencing [his client] to twelve years." The government's lawyer then told me that some of the victims were in court and wanted to be heard. The first one was Olivia. Her comments tracked her affidavit, and she identified herself as "the person who started in prostitution prior to my sixteenth birthday."

Others also spoke. I was particularly taken by what Maria said:

I am here because I want these people to be punished with a very stern sentence for them. I was badly hurt. They abused me, seduced me, abused me and tried to woo me. He wooed me so much only so that I would go work for him.

Aside from that, he played with my feelings. He toyed with my life. And he stepped on me as though I were garbage. He did not have the slightest consideration towards me, towards my daughters.

And frankly, I know they don't have the slightest idea what the value of a human being is. They don't care about destroying people's lives because what they want is money. What they want is to dominate the world by having a lot of women to themself. They feel like gods before a woman who has no defense because she's beaten and they totally mistreat them.

Gerardo then spoke. He refused to take any responsibility for his criminal misdeeds, in spite of his twenty-seven guilty pleas, starting off by saying that "my attorney knew that there is evidence and that I wanted to go to trial." He falsely accused me of not allowing him to change attorneys, and insisted that "[t]here is evidence that shows that I'm not guilty." As for one of the victims who had the courage to speak out against him, he said that "[e]verything she has said is a lie," and that she and the others "could go out at any time they wanted."

I came into court that morning mindful that the probation department had recommended thirty-five years of incarceration and that the low end of the advisory guideline range would probably turn out to be—as it did—thirty years. If I recalled correctly, I never before gave a sentence in excess of the probation department's recommendation.

While I always have a general sense of the likely sentence I will impose in any given case before coming into the courtroom after having read the presentence report, the probation department's comments, and the written submissions by the defendant's lawyer, I always reserve my final decision until I listen to everyone speak during the sentencing proceeding. The defendant's lawyer would usually make a compelling pitch for leniency and emphasize some of the good traits his client possessed, and I would usually give the defendant the benefit of the doubt. Ever since the guidelines became advisory, most of my sentences were below the low end of the range.

But as I listened to Gerardo continue to refuse to accept any culpability for any of the twenty-seven crimes to which he clearly had pleaded guilty, mindful of the defendants' disingenuous requests to change their pleas—after I had painstakingly made sure during their plea allocutions that they were voluntarily made—my stomach started to turn. If ever there would be a case where a defendant had deserved a sentence above what the government had recommended, this was it. After taking a deep breath, I explained why I would be sentencing Gerardo to fifty years:

> In imposing sentence, the Court considers the advisory guideline range of 360 months to life and also the factors set forth in 18 United States Code Section 3553(a). And in particular, the following aspects of that subsection. One, the nature and circumstances of the offense and the history and characteristics of the defendant.
>
> In that respect, the nature and circumstances of the offense I find to be appalling. We're not talking about one victim. We're not talking about two victims. We're talking about multiple victims that the defendant pled guilty to violating in a number of ways.
>
> And the Court doesn't have, as hard as I have searched, the proper words to express the Court's shock and disgust for the nature of the criminal behavior of this defendant. The Court cannot overlook and will not overlook the nature of the multiple charges and the pleas by the defendant to each and every one of those charges, the physical factors associated with them, the vulnerability of the victims and all of these other aspects that make these crimes horrendous.
>
> Now, the statute also speaks about the need for the sentence imposed to reflect the seriousness of the offense, to promote respect [for] the law and to provide just punishment for the offense. And also talks about the need to afford adequate deterrence to criminal conduct in the United States. I'm not going to

speak about Mexico. I have great respect for the country, Mexico. I can only talk about the laws of the United States which I am familiar with.

We do not condone the crimes that you have pled guilty to and sex trafficking, and all these other crimes that you have pled guilty to are things which, in this country of ours, we take a very, very dim view of.

And it's, I think, terribly important in particular in this case to send a message loud and clear that people—I don't care where they come from, whether they come from the United States, Mexico, any place—if they commit these crimes in the United States, they're going to be treated harshly by the law. We look upon these types of crimes amongst the most serious of crimes that can be committed.

The violation of women, the disrespect for women, all of these issues are matters which we take quite seriously in this country and our laws reflect that. And a stiff sentence is required here in my opinion to send a clear message that these types of criminal conduct will not be tolerated under our laws.

And, of course, you know, we want to protect the public from further crimes of this nature. There's nothing that suggests to me that the defendants would not return to their crimes. They have a hard time accepting responsibility for their acts here. We've discussed that at length and I think those factors all suggest that the Court must deal harshly in sentencing this defendant.

I don't see any particular history or characteristics of the defendant that weigh so heavily in his favor to grant the type of leniency that the defendant would like to have the Court visit upon [him].

I've considered all the factors under 3553(a), as well as the advisory guideline range and I think the reasonable sentence in this particular case is fifty years of incarceration.

It was then Josue's turn. He had changed lawyers. Roy Kulcsar was now representing him instead of Ted Del Valle, who I thought had represented him well. Kulcsar was an old war horse, and gave me right off the bat his practical take on my harsh sentence: "[I]t's hard considering that I spent many years prosecuting and trying murder cases and saw defendants who committed multiple murders getting twenty-five or thirty years to life, which is still the standard in the state."

I acknowledged that "I've imposed sentences where there have been deaths involved that were significantly less than what I'm doing here," and said that "I don't think my reputation is one of being the toughest sentencer on the bench." But I explained that "in this particular case" I thought that "this type of punishment was warranted" because of "the violation of women," the defendants' "whole modus operandi, the nature of the crimes, [and] their insensitivity to humankind."

Before I heard from Mr. Kulcsar's client, two other victims wanted to speak. Veronica was taken aback about the notion that fifty years would not also be an appropriate sentence for Josue because his lawyer had said he had not killed anyone, and emotionally cried out: "When I was pregnant, five months pregnant, when Josue arrived in New York he caused me to abort and as far as I'm concerned it was a killing that was not deserved for a human being to be killed in that way."

Emotions were in high gear as one other victim then spoke out, exclaiming that "[t]here are more women that this man has mistreated . . . whose lives have been destroyed for both the women and their families."

Like his brother, Josue was hardly repentant when he spoke. Moreover, in his view, he and his brother were "being judged for the most minimal things that we did." As I listened in dismay, I wondered what crimes he might have committed that were more serious than the ones to which he had confessed when he pleaded guilty and could not help reacting:

> [F]or you to characterize that you're being judged on the minimal things that you did sounds to the Court to be just bizarre in the face of your pleading guilty to twenty-seven serious crimes involving multiple, multiple victims and where you acknowledged that you caused physical harm to these people, as well as sex trafficking for the purposes of prostitution and everything else you pled guilty to.

And when you speak like this, it doesn't seem as if you're accepting the fact that you did confess to many crimes of the most serious nature here and you seem to want to diminish them and you had all the knowledge in the world before you pled guilty of your acts and your so-called wife and your situations that you speak about. And nonetheless, you pled guilty to all these crimes. You had every opportunity to go to trial and put forward a defense. You did not do that. You pled guilty. What else do you have to say?

He didn't have much else to talk about, and I could see no reason why he should not receive the same fifty-year sentence I gave his brother.

Daniel Perez Alonso was the last to be sentenced. His guideline range was also the same as his codefendants—thirty years to life. A new CJA lawyer—Charles Hochbaum—had been assigned to replace Alan Lashley, and he argued brilliantly on behalf of his client. He effectively pointed out significant differences between his client and the Carreto brothers. Daniel was only a susceptible, vulnerable seventeen-year-old when he became embroiled with the much-older Carretos, and he was significantly less culpable than they were in his interaction with the victims. Moreover, he had conducted himself admirably while he was in pretrial custody, as evidenced by a Bible study certificate that he had received from the prison.

And, most compelling was that, unlike the Carretos, he was contrite: He acknowledged that there were indeed victims, that "he was very sorry," and asked "for [my] forgiveness."

Hochbaum suggested a twenty-year sentence would be reasonable for Daniel. I gave him twenty-five—the same as the probation department's recommendation—which was five years below the low end of the advisory guideline range.

Although the sentences were over, the case was not. As the law required, I advised all the defendants of their right to appeal, and considering the heavy sentences I had handed out, encouraged them to do that. I would sleep better knowing that three appellate judges would sit in judgment of whether I acted appropriately in the way I handled the sentencing proceeding and the punishments I had rendered. But, short of being reversed and having the appellate court remand the case to me, I breathed a sigh of relief that I had seen the last of the Carretos—or so I thought.

On January 20, 2007, nine months after I had sentenced Gerardo, Josue, and Daniel—while the appeal was pending—Consuelo was extradited. I was back in business.

The feds had finally caught up with Gerardo and Josue's mother in Mexico, where she had been hiding out, and the Mexican government agreed that under the United States–Mexico Extradition Treaty, the three basic conditions that made an offense extraditable had been satisfied: (1) the criminal act was intentional; (2) the conduct charged was a crime in the laws of both countries, thereby meeting the double criminality standard; and (3) the crime was punishable with imprisonment of no less than a year.

The government worked out a plea deal with the mother, allowing her to plead to just the first count of the indictment, involving Jane Doe 1, in satisfaction of the rest of the charges. I accepted her plea because she confessed that this victim had lived with her in Mexico for about a year before her two sons took her to New York to work as a prostitute, and that she knew that monies that her sons sent to her were the proceeds of this victim's prostitution earnings.

The advisory guideline range for this conduct was 97 to 121 months. At her sentencing, her assigned counsel, John Wallenstein, made a very compelling statement on her behalf:

> Ms. Valencia was certainly a participant in this. I don't minimize that. But I believe that the true bad actors, as the Court has pointed out here, were her two sons. She is the person who received the sum of money, not all of it on her behalf. She did get some, and she's acknowledged that in her guilty plea.
>
> I believe that the Court, taking into consideration all of the factors in 3553(a), including her family which, unfortunately under the circumstances, is involved in this offense, but I'd ask

you to consider the fact that she is a mother. She lost a son to murder. She lost a husband. She lost a brother. And now she has lost her two surviving sons to the criminal justice system. She will never see them again. Your Honor gave them fifty years each. And even if she were free, it would be unlikely she'd be able to visit with them. So, she has lost everything she ever had and will now spend a substantial period of time in a federal penitentiary.

I'd ask you to consider all of that. Consider her age and her health. She's sixty-one years old and in poor health. I would ask you to consider all of those factors when you impose sentence.

Before I asked the defendant if she wished to be heard, two victims spoke to me. They each spoke about the abuses they suffered while living in her house. As one recounted: "She knew what was going on, and she allowed it. And, the times that she humiliated me and treated me worse than garbage, that's more than the humiliation. And, what she does is drag people, step on them, not caring what the people's feelings are."

Consuelo Carreto devoted her comments to attacking the victim's comments, and stood stoically in front of me as she concluded: "Your Honor, I'm in your hands. I tell you, before God, that what I'm telling you is the truth, and they have made all of this up. Everything they're saying is a lie, I swear."

Be that as it may, neither Consuelo nor her lawyer took issue with damning information contained in the presentence report, which recounted a number of numbing abuses she had committed on the women who she had harbored in her home, and concluded:

> Regarding her role in the instant offense, agents learned that the women clearly understood that Consuelo Carreto Valencia was the matriarch of the family. She resided in a much more luxurious home and virtually by her position in the family she commanded respect from the victims. Consuelo Carreto Valencia forced some of the victims to work as domestics in her home. She continuously told the women that they needed to

work more and needed to earn more money. At the same time, Consuelo Carreto Valencia told the victims that they were good for nothing but being whores. Consuelo Carreto Valencia financially benefited the most from the instant offense.

I sentenced the matriarch of the Carreto family to 121 months—the high end of the advisory guideline range, and explained why:

> My understanding of the law is that victims are entitled to speak to the judge. They're entitled to come to court. They're entitled to have the opportunity. But the law also instructs me that I am to base my sentence upon the record that has been established, and I can't take into consideration factually what the victims say. I think we have to be clear about that. They're not testifying under oath, but they are absolutely entitled to come here and speak. The law instructs me that the decision I render has to be based upon the record I have before me, and it does not include the statements of the victims.
>
> Based upon that record, I believe that the maximum of the advisory guideline range is clearly warranted. That's 121 months. There's a lot of information that's set forth in the presentence report that has not been controverted by the defendant. I'm not going to go through it step-by-step here. A lot of this is set forth in the comments that the probation department has set forth in their sentencing recommendation. But what dominates here, clearly, is just the nature of the crime that she has pled to. I think that clearly warrants the sentence at the high end of the guideline range.
>
> I think the record reflects my feelings about this type of crime. And under 3553(a), one can consider the nature of the crime here is heinous. It's just reprehensible. It's something that requires the maximum sentence that the guideline range recommends.
>
> As far as her personal characteristics are concerned, I considered that and all the factors under 3553(a)(1). I don't think I have to tick them off. I mean, she has hardly been the model

mother here. She has very little to commend her in terms of her personal characteristics.

I ended the sentencing proceeding by complimenting Mr. Wallenstein "for really doing an excellent job as the defendant's lawyer in difficult circumstances."

~

It took a while for the circuit court to render its decision on Gerardo, Josue, and Daniel's appeal, but Judge Chin, writing for a unanimous court, rejected all of their principal contentions. They all had argued that I should have allowed them to withdraw their guilty pleas and that I improperly considered their national origin in reaching my sentence. In addition, Daniel claimed I should not have denied his request to replace Lashley as his assigned counsel. The circuit court agreed that my decision in each of these situations was correct, and, of course, I was gratified.

I noted, however, that the defendants did not challenge the harsh sentences I had handed out. I assume they realized that there was no legal basis to do that since my sentences were technically all within the guidelines' ranges. I suppose I could have sentenced them to life—the upper end of the guideline range—without fear of reversal since no appellate court has ever reversed a sentence within the guideline range. But, upon reflection, I had some pains of conscience about the fifty years I gave the Carreto brothers. After all, neither the probation department nor the prosecutors had asked for a sentence above thirty-five years, and my initial take was that I would go along with that number. But the negative events that had unfolded during the sentencing proceeding just triggered my upping the ante. Even though I believed that under the law I should not be influenced by a victim's comments, I suspect that it was humanly impossible for me to subconsciously detach myself from what I heard from the mouths of the women whom the Carretos forced into prostitution and that I was not candid when I said that I would not consider the victim's comments.

I felt somewhat better about that when I realized afterward that I was not correct in my understanding of the law about the sentencing relevance of victim impact statements. While I believed that I could not consider victim impact statements in fixing my sentences, I based my belief on a Supreme Court decision that I did not realize had been reversed just a few years before. Today, not only are victims permitted to address the court, but also their comments are part of the sentencing mix that the judge can, and should, consider. As my colleague, the esteemed Judge Jack Weinstein cogently explained in one of his wonderfully crafted and insightful opinions:

> Victim impact statements and the sentencing desires of victims perform an important function in our modern criminal justice system. While a victim's reactions are not controlling, they are something that a judge must and should consider before imposing sentence. These statements serve three valuable purposes. First, they provide details about the seriousness of the crime. Second, they provide some indication of what punishment society deems appropriate. Finally, they allow victims to realize that they are important participants in the criminal justice process, thus preventing them from losing faith in the system and possibly turning to the dangerous course of self-help. Although the actual use of victim impact statements is somewhat recent, the role they play in the sentencing process has a long pedigree.

Sometimes I get way-out ideas while I'm sleeping. The night I finished sentencing the Carreto clan, it dawned on me during the middle of the night that I had sentenced them to a combined 135 years, plus one month, of incarceration. I knew that the annual cost to feed, clothe, and house an inmate in a U.S. jail was $30,000 and change. My curiosity got the best of me and I jumped out of bed to make the calculation. As I surmised, the cost of taxpayer monies to keep the Carretos in our jails would be in excess of $5 million. They were young enough *to probably not die before they served their time. They would then be deported back to Mexico.*

What a waste of money, I thought. Then the way-out idea hit me. Why not build a jail in Mexico and let them do their time there? It would provide needed construction and employment jobs for Mexicans, and keeping them in a Mexican jail would have to be a major cost-savings. I thought that the 5 million we will be spending on the Carretos here would go a long way toward building the first prison.

And the Carretos are just four of many prisoners populating our jails today who will be deported to their home countries immediately upon release. The vast majority of incarcerated criminals from south of the border come from Colombia and the Dominican Republic, in addition to Mexico. Jails could be built there also. Of course, we would need the cooperation of the authorities from those countries, but I could not imagine why they would not agree. As long as we could provide some oversight to make sure that the jails were properly and humanely run, we could have a significant reduction in our jail population, which could trigger a reallocation of our resources to deal with needed rehabilitation for our own criminals.

I realized, however, that this would probably be viewed as a harebrained idea and went back to bed, hoping that the Carretos would never again disturb my sleep.

4

Mandatory Minimums

John Doe

The Crime

Like the Carretos, John Doe also pleaded guilty to sex crimes. Because of the nature of the case—involving young children—I have decided not to disclose his real name. Unlike the Carreto brothers, where I could, and did, impose fifty-year sentences because there was no statutory limit to the maximum sentence I could render, the maximum sentence I could impose collectively for John Doe's two crimes was thirty years. It seemed, therefore, that the sex slavery crimes committed by the Carretos were viewed by Congress to be more serious than John Doe's. Or were they?

John's first crime, which carried the thirty-year max and a fifteen-year mandatory minimum, was for enticing a sixteen-year-old girl "to engage in sexually explicit conduct for the purpose of producing one or more images depicted in . . . computer files." The second crime, which carried a lesser maximum sentence of twenty years and had no mandatory minimum, was for possession of child pornography, after having downloaded pornography involving a twelve-year-old girl.

The plea of guilty was taken on February 2, 2015, by Magistrate Judge Vera M. Scanlon. Congress fixes the number of magistrate judges for each of the country's ninety-four districts and has created statutes governing the manner of their selection and their judicial responsibilities. They are appointed for eight-year terms by the districts' Board of Judges and can be reappointed by the district judges for additional similar terms until they reach seventy years of age.

Within the parameters established by Congress, the district judges carve out the magistrate judges' work responsibilities, which vary from district to district. In civil matters, they invariably prepare a case for trial by supervising all pretrial discovery; they may also try the case if the lawyers consent. In criminal matters, they may handle criminal arraignments and, if counsel consents, take pleas, which the district judge must review and approve; they may try misdemeanor cases, but not felony cases.

The magistrate judges are highly valued, and the work they do is indispensable to the management of the courts' dockets. The district judges select them purely on merit from a large, competitive pool of extraordinarily qualified candidates. Magistrate Judge Scanlon was one such candidate for this prized judicial position. She also had been one of my former law clerks.

I often joke that you know that "you're getting long in the tooth" when a former law clerk becomes a judge. When I learned that Magistrate Judge Scanlon would be taking the plea, it put a smile on my face. She was my first former law clerk who had made it to the bench. She beat out an exceptional field of candidates who had better credentials than I had when I was selected through the political system to become a district court judge. As we interviewed all the candidates, I thought to myself that the competition was so steep I probably would not have been selected by our board of judges as a magistrate judge if I had been a candidate, and I privately thanked the Lord that I had somehow made it through the White House and Senate selection process.

The judge who takes the plea must advise the defendant of the nature of the charges and of her or his rights. As expected, Magistrate Judge Scanlon did a superb job. She thoroughly explained to the defendant his constitutional rights, including that he did not have to plead guilty, even if he and everyone else might believe he was guilty, because the government must prove his guilt beyond a reasonable doubt. And she also told him about his right under the Fifth Amendment against self-incrimination—that if he chose not to testify at trial, no inferences could be drawn by the jury that he must be guilty. She also told him that recording having sex with a minor carried a mandatory minimum of fifteen years in jail.

Before a guilty plea can be accepted, the defendant must fess up to his crime since the judge must be certain that the defendant is not innocent and being coerced into pleading. Therefore, after Magistrate Judge Scanlon finished advising the defendant of his "rights," she told him, "It's not enough for you to say that you were guilty. You have to explain to me what it is that you did."

> THE COURT: Mr. Doe, what is it that you did such that you're guilty of [the two crimes]?
>
> JOHN DOE: I was in possession of child pornography and I had sex with a minor and it was recorded.
>
> THE COURT: When you say recorded, what does that mean?
>
> JOHN DOE: It was recorded through a computer.

In regard to the crime of recording having sex with a sixteen-year-old minor, the prosecutor explained that if the case went to trial, "the government is prepared to show . . . that the child was under the age of eighteen, through video of the child herself and witness testimony and documents as to the child's age. That the defendant used that child to engage in sexually explicit conduct for the purpose of producing a visual depiction of that conduct, through the video that shows . . . the defendant himself starting the recording and then engaging in the acts and using the child by engaging in a sexual act with her."

As for the downloading of pornography, the prosecutor explained that "the government would be prepared to show at trial that the defendant knowingly possessed a visual depiction and that visual depiction involved the use of a minor engaged in sexually explicit conduct. Evidence of that would be both the visual depiction itself, the evidence of a minor would be apparent from the depiction, as well as from the title of the videos and the knowing possession is apparent from agent testimony of the defendant's confession that he used the Internet to download the files, including the videos and possessed such videos on his computer."

Magistrate Judge Scanlon asked John Doe if the child "was not yet twelve years old?" He agreed. She then concluded the plea proceeding:

> **THE COURT:** All right. So for the record, based on the information given me, I find that . . . John Doe is fully competent and capable of entering an informed plea, that he's acting voluntarily, that he is aware of the nature of the charges against him, that he understands his rights and the consequence of his plea, and that there's a factual basis for the plea to both [counts] that's supported by an independent basis in fact as to each of the elements of the offense.
>
> So, I am to recommend, respectfully, that the district judge, Judge Block, accept the plea of guilty to [both counts] of the indictment.
>
> All right, with regard to sentencing, that date is going to be determined by probation in consultation with Judge Block's chambers.

On February 20, 2015, I reviewed the transcript of the pleas and signed a short order accepting it. I was satisfied that the defendant knowingly and voluntarily pleaded guilty to both crimes.

Even though I accepted the pleas, I did not know all the details of the crimes and was curious about a number of things, though none of them affected the validity of the pleas. First, I wondered why the defendant would be willing to plead to a crime that carried a fifteen-year mandatory minimum. I assumed he preferred to plead because the evidence was overwhelming and there was no realistic chance of a "not guilty" verdict. He probably thought that even though he would have to be sentenced to at least fifteen years, he would not get a higher sentence because he would get credit for "acceptance of responsibility." I also wondered whether he might have thought that I was not a tough sentencer, but if so, he may not have known about my fifty-year sentences for the Carreto brothers. I also was curious as to who the sixteen-year-old girl was and the age of the "under twelve-year-old girl" in the video he had downloaded. I also looked forward to receiving the presentence report (PSR) from the probation department to get all the specifics about the crimes and the defendant's personal history and characteristics to find out why the government wanted to put the defendant away for at least fifteen years. It seemed like a huge sentence.

I received the PSR on August 26, 2015, several months after the pleas. I learned that John Doe was a forty-year-old undocumented immigrant from Lima, Peru, and had been illegally living in the United States since 2003. It also told me that the sixteen-year-old girl was the daughter of the defendant's girlfriend.

In addition to giving me a lot of information about the defendant's personal life, the PSR gave me specific details about the crimes. I set October 30, 2015, for the sentence. But for an assortment of legitimate reasons there were a number of adjournments, and the sentence would not happen until 2018.

One of the reasons for the delay was because in March 2016, the defendant filed a pro se motion to withdraw his guilty plea and for the appointment by the court of a new lawyer. In a letter to me he complained that his retained attorney did not fully explain the plea to him and listed a host of other complaints he had about the quality of his legal representation. After discussing the matters fully with the defendant and his lawyer in court, I granted his requests and appointed Sally Butler to be his new attorney.

I selected Butler from the court's Criminal Justice Act list of approved attorneys to represent indigent defendants. Before I did that, I had decided that the defendant could no longer pay for private counsel and was entitled to a free court-appointed lawyer from the CJA list. Under the CJA, each district court is required to maintain a list of qualified attorneys who supplement the overworked federal defenders office. The EDNY has a CJA committee whose function is to screen and select lawyers for inclusion on the list. I used to be the chairperson of the committee, which is now skillfully chaired by Magistrate Judge Pollak, and the members are an assortment of judges, highly regarded criminal defense counsel, and leading layperson community representatives. The committee prides itself on selecting only highly qualified lawyers to represent the indigent. Sally Butler was one of those lawyers.

Butler went to work right away. She brought herself up to speed, retained a forensic psychologist, and quickly gained the defendant's trust. After many meetings with his new attorney, the defendant decided to keep to his plea agreement; thus, he accepted the fact that the mandatory minimum would require him to spend at least fifteen years in jail.

The Punishment

On May 25, 2017, the parties had appeared before me to discuss sentencing issues. In addition to the PSR, I had received letter submissions from both the government and the defendant's new attorney. Butler also submitted a psychological evaluation of the defendant by a consulting forensic psychologist, which concluded in the following:

> In essence, it is clear that John Doe has exercised extremely poor judgment in the recent past with respect to his stepdaughter and his Internet activities as it pertains to child pornography; how-

ever, at this juncture, there is no reason to believe that he is a predator—someone who cannot be trusted in the community or as someone who is preoccupied with making sexual contact with teenage girls and/or prepubescent children.

On this occasion the parties staked out their positions. Butler had submitted a letter from John Doe's girlfriend's daughter, who was now nineteen or twenty, "asking for the defendant to be released; that she recognized that she, too, had made a mistake and that the entire event had been consensual." And she also submitted a letter from her mother, who had sustained her relationship with the defendant and had regularly visited him in jail, asking that he be sent home to his "family."

I listened to Butler raptly as she made her pitch:

BUTLER: And of course, there is this culture difference. In Peru, the age of consent is fourteen, which doesn't make it legal here, but I think that it's mitigating circumstances in which a fifteen-year sentence, when this family just wants to be put back together again . . . and the so called victim is asking Your Honor to release this man.

The government's lawyer, Nathan Reilly, then explained why he thought the fifteen-year mandatory minimum was appropriate:

REILLY: Your Honor, I would say a couple of things. One, it is not a unique situation in which an abuser has a manipulative relationship and manipulated the feelings of . . . the victim. And I will call her a victim, because . . . the fact that there is a belief it's consensual, there is a reason that it's made illegal and that there is an age of consent. That's one.

THE COURT: One.

REILLY: Two . . . it's also significant the type of child—this was not a one-off, I fell in love with my girlfriend's daughter and I am culturally confused. He possessed graphic images of prepubescent girls that . . . indicates a sickness.

As I listened to the government's rationale for invoking the mandatory minimum, I was convinced that a significant amount of jail time was warranted but wondered whether fifteen years was over the top. I was truly troubled about where one draws the line between a rational and irrational sentence, and I wanted to ask a question that would engage the government's lawyer in that debate. I thought a somewhat sarcastic example might do it.

> **THE COURT:** Why not execute him?

The best Mr. Reilly could muster was that the government was "proceeding with the punishments that are set forth by Congress in its infinite wisdom." It triggered this response from me:

> **THE COURT:** We all know that fifteen years is an enormous amount of time. We all understand child pornography. . . . But fifteen years? We know people in jail for murdering people for fifteen years. . . . It does not mean we condone this behavior. It does not mean we are not going to punish it, but Congress imposes itself upon the discretion of the Court and it troubles us.

I ended the day by adjourning the sentence to allow Butler the opportunity to inquire whether the girl and her mother might wish to come to court to verbally reinforce their letters of support, and I asked the government's lawyer to talk to his superiors to see whether that might change the government's position about insisting on the fifteen-year mandatory minimum charge. In the interim, I was curious to find out about the evolution and current status of mandatory minimum statutes that Congress has enacted.

Congress enacted its first Crimes Act in 1790. It included twenty-three federal crimes, seven of which carried mandatory minimums—always death. The rest had only statutory maximums. It imposed the death penalty for treason, murder, three piracy offenses, rescue of a person convicted of a capital crime, and, surprisingly, forgery of a U.S. public security. Between that time and the Civil War era, Congress started to impose mandatory minimums for a range of noncapital cases for crimes ranging from manslaughter to horse stealing to bigamy. By the 1870s, at least 108 crimes had mandatory punishments, half of which were about income taxes. But when Congress enacted the Criminal Code in 1909, at least 31 were repealed.

Except for some mandatory minimums for alcohol-related offenses during Prohibition, Congress was pretty quiet for the first half of the twentieth century. Then, in the latter half, things started to really heat up. With the Omnibus Crime Control Act of 1970, Congress established a mandatory minimum for using a firearm during the commission of a felony, and with the Protection of Children Against Sexual Exploitation Act of 1977, the first mandatory minimum for child pornography came into existence. It was the beginning of a spate of congressional acts establishing mandatory minimums for a whole range of child pornography and sexual abuse cases leading to the passage of the Adam Walsh Child Protection and Safety Act of 2006, which created long periods of incarceration, including the fifteen-year mandatory term for the sexual abuse crime to which John Doe pled guilty. Coming down hard on these cases was the political way to go.

During the 1980s, Congress focused on drug offenses with the Anti-Drug Abuse Act of 1986 and the Anti-Drug Abuse Act of 1988.

The upshot of this mandatory minimum feeding frenzy was that by 2010 there were four basic categories of crimes that had caught Congress's attention: Drug trafficking led the pack with 77.4 percent of all such crimes carrying minimums, followed by sexual abuse (52.5 percent), child pornography (51 percent), and firearms (about 30 percent). There is no doubt that Congress had the right to do that. As the Supreme Court stated in *Chapman v. United States*: "Congress has the power to define criminal punishments without giving the courts any sentencing discretion."

In *Ewing v. California,* the high court noted that the only limit to the exercise of that power is the Eighth Amendment's prohibition against cruel and inhuman treatment, which "contains a 'narrow proportionality principle' that 'applies to noncapital sentences.'" But it explained that "successful challenges to the proportionality of particular sentences have been exceedingly rare." Thus, it "would . . . come into play in the extreme example . . . if a legislature made overtime parking a felony punishable by life imprisonment" but not, as in *Ewing,* when it imposed a sentence of twenty-five to life for a defendant convicted of his third felony, even though that felony was for stealing three golf clubs.

Whether a defendant will be charged with a crime carrying a mandatory minimum is a decision that is made by the U.S. Attorney's Office of each district in the exercise of its prosecutorial discretion. It will invariably be affected by the sociocultural and political climate in the district. In 2010, seven of the country's ninety-four districts accounted for 27 percent of cases involving convictions with a mandatory penalty: the southern and western districts of Texas, the southern and middle districts of Florida, the southern district of California, and the districts of Arizona and South Carolina.

Thus, the U.S. Attorney's Office in Brooklyn could have charged John Doe with a lesser crime that did not carry a mandatory minimum. But once it chose not to do that, it removed any discretion that the sentencing judge might otherwise have to impose a lesser sentence.

As I reflected on the sentence I would be imposing on John Doe, I wondered what the outer reaches might be under the Eighth Amendment for his crime. It seemed to me that Congress could do pretty much as it pleased. But what would be the cutoff line—twenty years, twenty-five years, or even life? Given the inordinate power of Congress to effectively take sentencing discretion away from the district court and the power of the U.S. attorneys to decide the crimes for which a defendant should be indicted, I realized that in fixing the sentence that must be imposed for a particular crime, coupled with the power of the U.S. attorneys to indict, the legislative branch had the power to reduce the sentencing judge to a mere functionary—except, I suppose, I could impose a sentence greater than the statutory minimum, though that is rarely warranted.

If it were up to me, I would leave sentencing in all cases strictly up to the judicial branch. And I did not like the fact that I had no discretion but to sentence John Doe to at least fifteen years.

On February 14, 2018, I sentenced the defendant to the fifteen-year mandatory minimum, even though the guidelines calculation was lower. The girl and her mother were there but chose not to speak, and the government did not budge. Before the sentence was officially imposed, the defendant spoke:

> I want you to forgive me, everybody here that's been involved in this. This is very hard for me. It is a mistake I made, and I now have to pay for it. I think you can see from the letters from my family the kind of person I am. But I am very, very repentant for this thing that I committed. Because now I can truly see the value of freedom and of having your family near you, and because my parents are very old right now. So I ask you for your mercy, but that's all. Thank you.

The defendant was truly contrite; he had no criminal history and was gainfully employed. Letters I had received from his family and employer spoke well of him. If not for the mandatory minimum, I probably would have imposed a lesser sentence, but while I had no choice, I ended the proceedings by expressing my dissatisfaction with the legislative branch's curtailment of my sentencing powers:

> It is the first fifteen-year mandatory I have had to dish out in twenty-three years. You know my feelings about it, but I am obliged to, of course, follow the law even if I don't approve of it here.

So there's not much more I can say about that. We have had a dialogue about this over the last several months. The time's come, and I have no alternative. I am satisfied he understands what's happened. He had a prior attorney who did everything he could to make sure his rights are fully guided and protected. And we're at the end of the line now, and we all have strong feelings about mandatory minimums. We generally don't like them because it imposes upon the sound exercise of the judge's discretion. Maybe I give him fifteen years in any event. But the fact is, it imposes upon the Court, by political people, you know, for reasons which may not be properly correlated with the concepts of justice, which is something that's abhorrent. Obviously, I am making this on the record because I strongly feel that way.

Of course, not all criminals are abusive to women. The Mafia are known to be protective of their families and the mothers of their children. If anything, they are overly fond of women. And as I learned in my one major mafioso trial, at least one Mafia chieftain's girlfriend was fatally attracted to him.

5

The Mafia

Peter Gotti and the Gambinos

The Crime

The impact of the federal government's use of RICO on the mob has been devastating. At its height, the Mafia had about two thousand "made" members nationwide. But its largest concentration was in New York and its metropolitan suburbs, where the Genovese, Luchese, Bonomo, Gambino, and Colombo families coexisted for half a century. By 1990, numerous RICO convictions against the families were having their intended effect. The head of the FBI's organized-crime branch in New York reported that although the Gambino and Genovese families were still functioning, "their power [was] dwindling." As for the other three New York families, he viewed them as "shattered and pretty well beaten."

A number of these convictions happened in my courthouse. The EDNY had long been viewed as an appropriate venue to try the leaders and members of New York's five Mafia crime families since they invariably lived within the EDNY—in either Queens, Brooklyn, or Staten Island—and did a lot of their dirty work there.

The most notorious Mafia chief was John J. Gotti, who was tried twice in the EDNY courthouse. He was the boss of the Gambino crime family from 1985 to 1992. In 1986, the FBI identified the Gambino family as the largest and most powerful Mafia family in the country, with four hundred to five hundred members. In 1984, just before he became the boss, Gotti had been acquitted in a state court trial. A refrigerator repairman named Ronald Piecyk had accused him of slapping him and taking $325 from him during a parking dispute in Queens. When he initially identified Gotti, Piecyk was unaware of his reputation as a mobster. But he knew who he was at the time of the trial. On the witness stand, a tense Mr. Piecyk had a sudden lapse of memory and could no longer recognize Gotti. The judge had no choice but to dismiss the case.

In 1987, a jury acquitted Gotti of federal RICO charges in the first case against him in the EDNY. Judge Nickerson was the judge. The foreman of the jury was later convicted of accepting a $60,000 bribe arranged by Sammy the Bull Gravano—Gotti's underboss—to vote to acquit. It was the most stinging courtroom defeat suffered by the government in its campaign against the Mafia. Law enforcement officials grudgingly conceded that John Gotti's back-to-back acquittals had wrapped him in a perceived cloak of invincibility.

In 1990, Gotti was brought to trial in state court in Manhattan on an indictment charging him with ordering the shooting of a carpenters' union president after a labor dispute. Again he was acquitted, despite secretly recorded tapes in which he was heard discussing preparations for the shooting and despite damning testimony from a participant in the plot. Later, a New York City police officer assigned to the investigation was convicted on charges of being employed by the Gambino family and had given it the names and addresses of the jurors. John Gotti was now a celebrity criminal and became known as the "Teflon Don."

But the Teflon Don's luck finally ran out that year. The FBI had secretly bugged an apartment above his hangout, the Ravenite Social Club. For several months, the bugs recorded conversations that implicated him and others in a host of crimes, including murder. He was arrested in December 1990 and charged under RICO for murder, conspiracy, gambling, obstruction of justice, and tax fraud. The case was his second trial in the EDNY. This time Judge Glasser was the judge. In April 1992, the Teflon Don was convicted on all counts and sentenced to life in prison. His conviction was sealed by the testimony of his right-hand man, the turncoat cooperator Sammy the Bull.

In 2002, John Gotti died in jail of cancer at the age of sixty-one. After Gotti was imprisoned, his son "Junior" became the Gambino family boss. The apple did not fall far from the criminal tree, and in 1999 Junior pleaded guilty to racketeering and extortion charges. He was sentenced that year to seventy-seven months in prison. According to the government, Peter Gotti—the Teflon Don's older brother—then became the acting boss of the Gambino crime family. His buddies affectionately called him Uncle Peter.

It took the government three years to get the goods on Uncle Peter. It believed that he clung to power in the Gambino crime family as a way to keep the Gotti clan in control of millions of dollars of criminal proceeds. Fed up with the Gambino's continued criminal misdeeds—especially its corrupt control of the main longshoreman's union that ran the New York waterfront—the government swept broadly to try to deliver a fatal blow to the family. In 2002, it indicted Peter Gotti and sixteen others in a sixty-eight-count indictment. In essence, the government charged the defendants under RICO with being Gambino family members engaged in racketeering schemes involving labor unions and businesses operating at piers and terminals in Brooklyn and Staten Island by extortion, illegal gambling, wire fraud, and money laundering.

The only one of these crimes that Uncle Peter was charged with was money laundering, meaning that monies from the enterprise's criminal misdeeds were funneled to him. But the government also charged him with racketeering and racketeering conspiracy under RICO because it believed that the monies were given to him because he was either the acting or actual boss of the Gambino crime family. As such—under RICO—he was deemed to have condoned all of the crimes committed by the codefendants, including the extortions. One of the extortion charges was that a Gambino captain and his underling threatened to kill the martial arts actor Steven Seagal if he did not pay them $3 million.

Since Judge Glasser had handled the trial that resulted in the conviction of the Teflon Don, the government had the case assigned to him. At that time, it could pick the judge if it believed that the new case was somehow related to a prior case that the judge had presided over. The prosecutor's office was obviously happy to have Judge Glasser. The government had also steered a number of other successful Mafia racketeering prosecutions his way. But Judge Glasser had his fill with Mafia trials and thought that a single judge should not preside over all of the Mafia cases. He insisted that the case be put in the criminal wheel for random assignment. I got it.

Peter Gotti was arrested and jailed on June 4, 2002. On August 10, I denied his application to be released on bail pending his trial, which would not take place for several months. Six days later, the prison warden took him out of the general prison population and placed him in administrative detention. This meant that Peter would be confined to a tiny cell with only a metal bed; there was no TV or any other amenity. He would be let out just one hour a day during the week—but not on the weekend—to walk around a little. The warden thought Peter should be locked down after the FBI had informed him that the Gotti family had threatened to kill the warden of the jail where John Gotti had been housed for allegedly mistreating his younger brother before he died.

On September 2, Peter's lawyer, Gerald Shargel, asked me to order that his client be placed back into the general population. He argued that there was no basis to the threat and it was illegal to punish Peter while he was in jail waiting for his trial. The issue was a serious one. As a pretrial detainee, Peter was entitled to the presumption of innocence. Under the Constitution, he could not be punished by being locked down in the absence of a credible reason. I thought the right thing to do was have a factual hearing so that the government could tell me why he should remain in isolation.

To guard against any confidential information getting out, I held the hearing *in camera*—in my private chambers—and ordered that the transcript be placed under seal. The government's lawyers informed me that the FBI told them that it had not concluded that there was any basis to the death threat but it needed more time to complete its investigation. I asked them to find out how much time it would need and told them to report back to me by the end of the week. When I did not get a response, on September 10 I ordered that Peter's lockdown end. He had now been kept in deep freeze for just about one month.

The government took issue with my decision and got a stay from the circuit court of appeals pending a full argument before the appellate court. This did not happen until October 7. In the meantime, Peter Gotti remained locked down in his tiny cell. At the argument, his lawyer repeatedly told a three-judge panel that it was unconstitutionally punitive to keep "a presumably innocent man in a box, twenty-three hours a day and twenty-four hours on weekend[s]," with no relief in sight, based upon unconfirmed rumors. One of the panel members was then circuit court judge Sonia Sotomayor. (She had no idea that years later she would be appointed to the Supreme Court.) When the government's lawyer, Andrew Genser, rose to speak, Judge Sotomayor immediately said Gotti's lawyer was "absolutely right" and asked rhetorically, "Why isn't it punitive?" Genser never gave her a satisfactory answer. He argued instead that the Prison Litigation Reform Act prevented judicial review of the conditions of confinement for a pretrial detainee.

The appellate court was not impressed. Although it reserved decision, it was pretty apparent to courtroom observers that it would come down hard on the government. The *New York Law Journal* reported the next day that the judges "aggressively challenged Assistant U.S. Attorney Andrew Genser to justify the isolation of Mr. Gotti from other inmates" and "made the prosecutor work hard to back up his contention that the Prison Litigation Reform Act prevents judicial review."

Seeing the handwriting on the wall, the warden put Gotti back into the general population on November 10—before the court came down with its decision. By doing so, he was able to dodge the judicial bullet since the court then held that the issue was now moot. I thought that Judge Sotomayor and her colleagues should nonetheless have addressed the merits and taken the government to the woodshed. Regardless of what people may have thought about the Gottis, it was unconscionable for the government to keep him locked up like an animal for one-third of a year for no supportable legitimate reason.

The trial started on January 14, 2003. Nobody, except me and my staff, knew the names or addresses of the jurors. Knowing of the Mafia's history of jury tampering, I decided that the jurors should be anonymous. This is not normally the case, but I could do that if I concluded, as I did, that there was strong evidence to believe the jury needed protection. The prospective jurors would each be referred to by number. The 12 jurors and alternates were selected from a group of 501, who were required to answer a forty-seven-page questionnaire. While every effort was undertaken to protect their anonymity, they had to reveal some personal information, such as their marital status, income, and hobbies, to give the lawyers a fair shot at exercising their peremptory challenges. From this group, the lawyers for both sides agreed that 200 should be excused for cause. The main reasons were that they were either biased against the Mafia or were too frightened to sit, given the mob's well-earned reputation for violence. Those who were not excused were called into the courtroom in the order of their number and questioned by me to determine whether they could give both sides a fair shake and base their verdicts solely on the evidence. Ultimately, the requisite twelve jurors—and a number of alternates—were selected.

I tried my best to assure them that every effort had been made to ensure their safety. They would not be locked up overnight, but if they wished they could be picked up and taken home by court marshals. They had to promise me, however, that they would not let any biases or fears prevent them from being fair and objective. I also told them that they were not to read anything about the case in the newspapers or watch TV reports. If they saw or heard anything, they were to report it at once to the court's clerk. I tried to impress upon them that the case was to be tried in the courtroom—not in the press—and only the evidence presented during the trial could be considered by them.

Picking a jury in a high-profile Mafia case is a tall order. No matter how hard I tried, there was no escaping the reality that the jurors knew what they were in store for. Any Gotti trial would be a feeding frenzy for the media—especially one where a movie star was in the mix—and the jurors would have a hard time staying focused and fearless. I think I picked a good jury and hoped the Gambino family would not find out who the jurors were.

As I was picking the jury, I recalled that this was not the first time I was involved in selecting a jury in a Mafia case. One day—during my prior life as a lawyer—Ray Kirchoff walked into my office and told me he had just been indicted in Nassau County on a bunch of perjury counts for lying before a grand jury that was investigating a Mafia murder. He could not understand why "they were picking" on him and why he was "hauled before the grand jury." He told me he ran a legitimate used car business but that a number of his customers were mafiosi. He thought they were nice guys and that he would occasionally loan them cars.

After listening to Ray regale me with mafiosi stories, I told him to stop being cute with me. He obviously understood why the Nassau DA wanted to ask him some questions before the grand jury—after all, the victim's body was found in the trunk of one of his cars.

Ray Kirchoff was a colorful guy, and even though he was obviously a wannabee mafioso, he was charming, respectful, and a good client. And he always promptly paid his legal fees—in cash. I had handled an assortment of run-of-the-mill criminal cases in my general practice—and a few assigned-counsel murder cases—but this would be my first perjury trial.

The trial lasted just a few days, but the jury deliberated for much longer. Ray never outright lied, but I had to explain to him that he could still be found guilty if the jury believed that his "I don't remem-

bers" and "I don't knows" were disingenuous and obviously evasive. After three days, the jury reached a verdict. It was pretty exciting stuff, as the jury foreperson said "not guilty" to each of the first six counts. We were ready to celebrate, but, lo and behold, she meekly blurted out "guilty" on the last of the seven-count indictment.

It was obviously a compromise verdict. The jurors had been hung and rendered their verdict only after the judge had told them that if they were unable to reach one, the case would have to be retried before another jury. On balance, things could have been worse and Ray was only sentenced to thirty days in the county jail. I sensed that he was not unhappy about it and that he probably thought his reputation with the "boys" would go way up for taking one on the chin for them. As things turned out, he was right.

Peter Gotti turned to look at an attractive middle-aged blonde sitting in the third row of the courtroom's visitor section as the government's opening remarks were delivered by Assistant U.S. Attorney Rick Whelan. He and two other AUSAs—Genser and Katya Jestin—would be the prosecutorial team. Whelan had a low-key but forceful style. He told the jury that the government would prove through tapes and videos that Peter became the Gambino family boss after Junior Gotti went to jail, and that as the boss, he took a cut of the proceeds of the monies his codefendants Anthony Cicone, Primo Cassarino, Jerome Broancato, and Richard Bondi (appropriately known as "the Lump") had extorted from innocent victims through shakedowns on the docks in Brooklyn and Staten Island. Whelan said that the other two codefendants, Peter's brother Richard V. Gotti and his nephew Richard G. Gotti, were intermediaries who funneled the cash to Peter. Whelan acknowledged that Peter did not participate in any of the extortions—and was only charged with money laundering—but because he was the boss, he should also be found guilty of racketeering.

Whelan laid out a number of other crimes that Peter's codefendants had committed. The most striking was the government's charge that Cassarino and Cicone tried to shake down Seagal at the behest of the actor's former producer—an alleged Gambino family associate—to pay the family $150,000 for each film he made. Whelan told the jury that the actor would testify and said, "You'll hear them laugh at how scared Seagal was at one of the meetings," on tapes that had been secretly recorded. I knew right then that this would be a major media event. The jurors would hear the macho martial arts film celeb cowering in fear of his life.

In their opening statements, the defendants' lawyers cautioned the jurors to keep an open mind and told them that while they would hear the defendants use lots of four-letter words on the tapes, they should not be convicted for not speaking the queen's English. In the final analysis, they told the jurors that there would be a reasonable doubt as to their clients' guilt.

Peter's lawyer took particular pains to caution the jury not to punish his client because he was a Gotti. Shargel told them, "The presence of John Gotti in this courtroom will be palpable," and said that Peter was a proxy for the prosecutors trying to milk more mileage out of his late brother's notoriety. His defense was simple. Peter was not the boss of the Gambino family. He was just a retired sanitation worker living off a disability pension and Social Security. Shargel drew a chuckle from some of the jurors when he said, "When Mario Puzo wrote *The Godfather*, he did not have Peter Gotti in mind." He drove home his point by telling them that, "No actor on *The Sopranos* plays Peter Gotti."

The battle lines had been drawn. In order to convict Peter Gotti of racketeering, the prosecutors would have to convince the jurors that he was indeed the acting or actual Gambino boss. They would have to do this by proving that he knowingly associated with the Gambino family and conducted or participated in the affairs of that criminal enterprise.

Ray Kirchoff certainly knowingly associated with the Mafia, and some of the boys wanted to show their appreciation for not squealing on them. One morning, just a few days after he got out of jail, he popped into my office on Main Street in Smithtown to tell me that we were going to the city to have lunch with his buddies to celebrate; he insisted that I come and would not take no for an answer.

As I was getting ready to leave, my good friend Judge Morton Weissman stopped by. He had just finished his court calendar for the day and wanted to treat me to lunch. I introduced him to Kirchoff, who invited the judge to join us for lunch in New York City. I asked Morty to do me a favor and come with me. He probably shouldn't have, but he was a good guy and would not abandon a friend in need.

I drove my car and at Ray's direction parked in a no-parking zone right in front of Angelo's on Mulberry Street. As we got out of the car, we were met by an entourage of five well-built guys who kissed and hugged Ray and then led us into the restaurant. One of them told me not to worry about the car, and the eight of us sat down at a big round table next to the front window. I was told by another one of our "hosts," who said his name was "Blackie," that it was "the most important table in da joint."

Soon after we sat, a waiter brought a large bottle of Chianti, filled all the wineglasses, and stood at attention as one of the five macho men proposed a toast "to Ray and his Jewish lawyer." I tried not to squirm in my chair, and I thanked him for complimenting me for "doing a great job in getting Ray off." Nick the chef then came out of the kitchen carrying a giant meat cleaver and told us he had prepared a special feast for the occasion.

When Ray told the gang that my friend was a Suffolk County Court judge, I thought that Morty was going to faint, and I felt badly for talking him into coming with me. But he was a good sport and tried to make some friendly conversation. Blackie reciprocated and couldn't resist telling the judge that he, too, was celebrating because he had also just got out of jail. Morty made the fatal mistake of asking him what he "was in for." Blackie couldn't resist and shot back, "For moider." He got the hoped-for reaction from the suddenly pale-faced judge, who later learned that it was "only for extortion."

Blackie was not done. When the good judge got up after the second of seven courses had been served and the wineglasses had been filled for the third time, Blackie asked him where he was going. Morty sheepishly told him he was going to call his wife to tell her that he might be late for dinner and not to worry. "Judge, sit down," Blackie playfully barked. "You Jewish guys don't know how to treat da broads. I'm also married, but I know how to handle the wife. When we came back from da honeymoon in Vegas, I told her the first morning that I was goin' out to get the paper and would be back soon. When I came back three weeks later, she asked me where I was. I whacked her one and asked her, Where did I say I was goin'? She said to get the newspaper. I said dat's right, and don't ever ask me again. She never did. Now I ain't gonna let you call da wife."

We got home at 11 o'clock that night. Morty's wife didn't speak to him for three days. Neither did mine.

The government tried to establish that Peter was the boss right out of the chute with its first witness, FBI Special Agent Greg Hagarty. AUSA Genser—who had locked horns with me over my ruling that there was no legitimate basis to keep Gotti in deep freeze—questioned him. Genser had called Hagarty as an expert on the structure and organization of the Mafia. He had acquired his expertise over a number of years in the course of the many Mafia investigations he had conducted. This type of testimony was permissible for general background purposes to explain to the jurors the hierarchy of the Mafia's families. Hagarty could educate the jurors, for instance, as to the roles of the bosses, captains, consiglieres, and soldiers, and about the type of criminal activities the families engaged in. But Genser had more in mind, and when he asked Hagarty if he knew who the boss of the Gambino family was, Shargel shot to his feet to object before the question could be answered. Hagarty was obviously going to finger Peter Gotti.

Shargel's objection was well taken. I excused the jury while I asked Hagarty if he had any personal knowledge that Peter Gotti was the boss. He candidly said he did not but that it was generally understood that he was. I sustained the objection. Hagarty's answer would be pure hearsay. His testimony had to be limited to his knowledge of the general organization and practices of the Mafia.

Genser was upset and took me on. He told me that Hagarty had testified in John Gotti's case before Judge Glasser and was permitted to tell the jury that the Teflon Don was at that time the Gambino boss. To rub it in, he said that all of the other judges who had tried Mafia cases had allowed Hagarty to name the bosses. I said I would not allow that to happen in this case because here the issue of whether Peter Gotti was the boss was the central issue of the racketeering charges against him. The government would have to establish that Peter was the boss through the testimony of someone with personal knowledge.

Genser tried to do this two days later by calling Michael D'Urso to the stand. D'Urso had been a Genovese crime family associate and was a mob informant who had testified in a number of organized-crime cases. But D'Urso also told me that he, too, had no direct knowledge that Peter Gotti was the Gambino boss. His only knowledge came from an unidentified Genovese soldier who told him after John Gotti and Junior had been imprisoned that Peter had told him that he had risen from acting boss of the Gambino family. Peter's exact words were—according to the soldier—"I'm not acting. I'm official. I run this family." This, too, was hearsay, but under the rules of evidence, it could nonetheless be admissible if D'Urso and the Genovese soldier were involved in the events that were at the center of the government's case. They were not.

Genser would not give up. He asked me three times to reconsider my ruling barring D'Urso's testimony, as well as Hagarty's. In an effort to appease him, I relented to the extent that I would allow Hagarty to testify about the status of people not on trial. In a prickly exchange, I told him, "You've got to have better evidence than that to justify a conviction." He shot back, "Obviously we have, Your Honor."

Proving the adage that no good deed goes unpunished, the next day the *Daily News* reported that because I had modified my ruling about Hagarty's testimony, the feds were concerned about my "decision-making style." It also reported that "a senior law enforcement official familiar with yesterday's ruling complained that Block apparently failed to grasp parts of D'Urso's testimony." I do not know who these unidentified sources were, but the comments were obviously designed to paint me in a negative light. They were cheap shots. They were also totally unprofessional because these out-of-court statements by the government could prejudice the jurors if they saw them. I hoped Genser had no part of it, but I braced for a war.

It did not happen. Things calmed down, and the next several days the government played tons of tapes it had obtained over the years from cell phone intercepts and the bugs it had planted in the social club. The intercepted conversations were between most of the defendants and went a long way to proving the government's case against all of them. Peter Gotti was not in any of them, but there were some conversations that would give the jury the opportunity to infer that he was indeed the boss.

The tapes gave the jurors a poignant taste of how the defendants spoke to each other. For sure, the queen's English was never spoken. To the contrary, every conversation was laced with profanity. It made for some awkward moments. For example, the courtroom is open to all. I can only bar the public from listening to the trial if there are real safety reasons. Cursing is not one of them. When I came to court on the morning of Friday, February 14, there were six high school students from Bronx Morris High School sitting in the public seats. They were on a school-sanctioned field trip and obviously thought the Gotti trial would be worth the trip. But they got an earful when the government played tapes of Cassarino spewing obscenities at an alleged loan sharking victim. I squirmed in my chair as they heard him bellow:

> I don't give a fuck if the FBI is listening. You're pushing your motherfucking luck. I don't give a fuck about the law. Ya know what you are? You're a greaseball fuckin' scumbag, that's what you are. You're a greaseball, no-good motherfucker.

Peter Gotti—concerned that the students would have a bad impression of him—immediately turned to them and said, "That's not me cursing on the tape." Later, outside the courtroom, Shargel was reported as having told the press, "We haven't heard a tape with

Peter Gotti's voice on it." And Richard Levitt, Cassarino's lawyer was quoted as saying—in the understatement of the year—that the students "heard language in the courtroom that they don't normally hear in the classroom." I invited the students to my chambers during the morning break to give them an opportunity to talk to me. They assured me that it was not the first time they had heard this type of language. They thanked me for letting them listen in. They told me they were riveted by this real-life courtroom drama. Five of them said they wanted to become lawyers.

There were other real-life experiences. One day I walked into the public elevator coming back to court after lunch. At that time there was no private judges' elevator because the courthouse was under renovation. I had no choice. It was either take the elevator or walk up four flights of stairs to the courtroom. But as the elevator door was closing, in walked "the Lump." He was the least culpable defendant. His only alleged crime was that he helped Cassarino collect an extortionate debt that was owed to the family. His role was simply to stand in the doorway of the victim's house—all four hundred pounds of him—while Cassarino told the poor guy who opened the door that he "better pay up or else." Obviously the Lump was the "else." The debt was paid on the spot.

Because of his limited role, the Lump was out on bail. He was free to come and go as he pleased. It was easier for him to take the elevator than to risk a heart attack by walking up the stairs. No one else came into the elevator. In one sense, it was a good thing. The Lump took up so much space, anyone else would have had to squeeze in. I thought of that guy who paid up as soon as he saw him. Sensing my discomfort, the Lump tried to put me at ease by telling me, "You'se a good judge. We all like you and have a lot of fuckin' respect for you. Otherwise, I would squash you like an ant." I wondered what he would have said if I had let Agent Hagarty testify the way Genser wanted him to.

The Lump was not the first humongous mafioso I had met. I was practicing law on my own for about a year when I formed a partnership with Bob Burns. He was much older than I and had a nice little estates practice and a quaint office on Main Street in Port Jefferson. There was a spare room that I moved into and where I brought the few clients I managed to get throughout the year. One of them was the Nobi Carting Company. I had met its owner, Don Weiss, at the local synagogue. He was new in town and had just bought the carting company from a local who had been picking up the Village's garbage for several years. Don was concerned that the mob had its eyes on the Suffolk County carters because it had been buying up a number of routes in the western part of the county, and he convinced many other local carters to band together. He asked me if I would incorporate them. The Suffolk County Cartmen's Association was the first not-for-profit association I incorporated.

One bright summer day, while I was sitting at my desk waiting for the phone to ring, in walked Fat Angelo Garofalo. He weighed more than the Lump. He said he was the new president of the Association and was here to "pick up all da files." It didn't take me very long to give them to him.

The next day, Don told me he was selling Nobi Carting and asked me if I would handle the legal work. I was surprised. He had built up the business during the year and it was booming. Don told me that "discretion was the better part of valor," and he really had no choice. He asked me to come to the Limongellos' home in Lindenhurst for the closing the next day. I asked him who had prepared the contract. He said, "No one, none was needed. They just need a lawyer there."

When we arrived at the Limongellos', we were met at the door by Mama Limongello, who was super friendly and took us down to the basement. "Blind Joe" and his brother were there with Sal Ribando. I recognized Sal at once—he was the manager of the local branch of Security National Bank where I had my accounts. Everyone was very cordial. Sal had a bill of sale with him and other documents that he said my "client" had to sign and asked me if I would simply notarize Don's signature.

After the paperwork was done, Sal handed Don a check for $100,000 and had the Limongellos sign a series of promissory notes in that amount made payable to the bank. The Limongellos and Don shook hands, and Mama Limongello told everyone that it was time to "mangia."

I sat next to Sal Ribando at the sumptuous feast. The pasta was the best I had ever tasted, and the brothers kissed their mom and complimented her on the magnificent Limongello sauce, "made from an old secret family recipe from scratch." As I got up to leave—and thanked everyone for their over-the-top hospitality—I naively asked Sally (as the Limongellos called him) what security the bank had for the money it had loaned the Limongellos. Without missing a beat, he whispered, "All the security we need."

And then there was the day when Betsy, who would eventually become my second wife, came to court. There was not a day during the trial when the defendants' wives did not come. The lawyers had pointed them out to the jurors during the course of the trial. It was their way of showing that they supported their husbands. They sat together in the second row on the right side of the aisle. But the lawyers never mentioned who the women were who were sitting in the third row on the other side of the aisle. They also came to court each day. They were considerably younger than the wives and generally more attractive. They had a certain suggestive look—long blond hair, tight skirts, high heels. Many of them wore sunglasses. I remember from *The Godfather* movies how family-oriented the mafiosi were. They would never divorce their wives and were admirably protective of their families. But this did not prevent them from having women on the side. I was told by the marshals that they believed the women in the third row were some of the defendants' girlfriends.

Betsy did not know this when she came into the courtroom during the first week of the trial to see what was happening. She unwittingly sat in the third row. In my biased opinion, she was more appealing than the women who surrounded her, but with her Cartier aviator sunglasses, long blond hair, high heels, and miniskirt, she fit right in. Months after the trial had ended, I ran into Peter Gotti's lawyer at a bar association function. Shargel told me that Betsy had created quite a stir. The boys did not know who she belonged to. They thought they knew all the girlfriends and were annoyed that someone was holding out. The ones who had girlfriends each swore that Betsy was not their other woman. No one believed anyone. Cassarino thought she must have been Peter's and accused him of cheating on his regular girlfriend. Shargel finally made peace by telling the gang that the mystery woman was the judge's girlfriend. They were astonished—but they told Shargel that their respect for the judge just went right through the "fuckin' roof."

Peter did indeed have a girlfriend—the blonde he had looked at when the government began its opening statement. I knew who she was because she introduced herself to me one day while I was having lunch at the local Greek diner. She told me her name was Marjorie Alexander and that she was the woman sitting every day on the far end of the third row. I told her I could not talk to her, but she insisted on telling me that she and Peter had been together for many years and were madly in love with each other. Although I cut the conversation short, it did not end there. It seemed like every day I would get a letter from Marjorie telling me everything about her life with Peter and how much she was in love with him. I kept them in the court's file. Little did I know then what she would do after the trial was over.

At the beginning of the fourth week of the trial, Steven Seagal took the witness stand, raised his right hand, and swore to tell the truth. The courtroom was packed. There were reporters all over the place—many from L.A.—who were chomping at the bit to write about Seagal's involvement with the Gambino family. The fifty-eighth count of the indictment charged Cassarino and Ciccone of conspiring to extort money from the movie star, and the fifty-ninth count charged them with actually attempting to do that. They were not the most important charges in the case—and had nothing to do with Peter Gotti or the Gambino family's control of the waterfront—but they certainly brought out the crowd.

Conscious of his public persona, Seagal—with his painted hairline and red bracelets dangling from his neck—was clad in a chocolate-brown silk kimono, jeans, and construction boots. He testified that he was licensed to carry a gun and always carried one when he was in New York. I made sure he did not have one with him in court. He had just flown back from Thailand—where he was making his latest movie, *Belly of the Beast*—for his court appearance. He described himself as an "actor, producer, director, musician, songwriter." At first he was very combative, befitting a self-proclaimed martial arts expert. But under aggressive cross-examination, his testimony started to get shaky and evasive. I told him he had to be more responsive: "Listen to me. I don't have any experience in martial arts, but I have other powers here. Just listen to the question and answer it." I then took an early lunch break "so people can cool off a little bit." When he came back into the courtroom for continued cross-examination, his tough-guy image was totally shattered. He brought two red shawls with him and asked me if he could place them over his lap to warm his chilly knees. The audience laughed.

In his testimony, Seagal told the jury that he had a sit-down with Cassarino and Ciccone in a private room at Gage & Tollner, a popular restaurant in downtown Brooklyn. His one-time best friend and former producer, Jules Nasso, was with him. Nasso had ties to the Mafia and enlisted Ciccone to resolve an ongoing dispute he had with Seagal over money that Nasso claimed the movie star owed him. Seagal told the jurors that Ciccone began talking to him about "monies that I owed Jules" and "went into the fact that he wanted me to work with Jules." Seagal told Ciccone he was trying, at which point Ciccone ordered him to "look at me when you are talking." Ciccone then said: "Look, we're proud people and work with Jules. . . . Jules is going to get a little and the pot will be split up. . . . We'll take a little."

The meeting ended with Seagal stating that "he would try to work with Jules." Seagal testified that as he walked out of the restaurant, Jules walked with him and said, "You know, it's a good thing you said this and didn't say that because if you would have said the wrong thing, they were going to kill you." Seagal told the jurors that he had broken his relationship with Nasso because Nasso was using mood-elevating drugs and "going into psychotic rages." Nonetheless, he testified that he paid Nasso between $500,000 and $700,000—he was not very good with numbers—after he escaped with his life.

As Seagal recounted his real-life adventure, he seemed to regain his composure and warmed to the audience. He began making dramatic faces—complete with his famous furrowed brow—in response to questions. He grinned at a juror. When he finished his testimony and I told him he could step down, he bowed twice to the crowd and said, "Thank you all." The media event was over. It was time to get back to the rest of the trial.

The trial lasted for about another month. On March 5, I charged the jury. Because there were so many counts and defendants, my written instructions were 119 pages long. I had to explain to the jurors the law that applied to each of the sixty-eight counts and tell them which defendants were charged in each count. Although they were all charged in the two racketeering counts, they were not all implicated in the other sixty-six counts. Moreover, there were thirty-three racketeering acts that were the underlying predicates for the racketeering charges. Not all the defendants were alleged to have participated in each of these acts. The jury had to sort it all out and decide whether each defendant had committed at least two of these racketeering acts within the last ten years before they could convict a defendant on the RICO charges. It was complicated stuff.

I gave the jury copies of the charge as a guide, but since the law required me to also deliver it orally, I spent the entire day doing that. We took a brief lunch break and other mini-breaks throughout the day to stretch and use the bathrooms. As was my practice, I stood before the jurors. I did not read the charge verbatim. I varied from the script many times to more fully explain what was on the written page. I tried to make as much eye contact with the jurors as possible to keep them alert. I felt sorry for them. It was a tedious process. At the end of the day, everyone was exhausted. I had lost my voice.

The jury deliberated for the better part of the next two weeks before they informed the marshal sitting outside the jury room that it had reached a verdict. Since the jurors had to decide whether each of the racketeering acts had been proven, the verdict sheet was forty pages long. The jury unanimously found each of the defendants guilty of the racketeering counts. Nonetheless, the jurors were very responsible. They carefully went through each racketeering act and found that the government had not proven a number of them: it had proven enough of them, however, to warrant the racketeering convictions. The jury also found some of the defendants not guilty on the other counts.

As Peter Gotti was led out of the courtroom to be sent back to jail, he grumbled, "Gottis are easy to convict. All you have to have is the name." I thanked the jurors for their extraordinary public service. The marshals escorted them out of the courtroom. The trial for them was over. I, however, was hardly finished. I would have to decide how to sentence each defendant.

The Punishment

It took the next several months to prepare for the sentences. The probation department had to prepare a lengthy presentence report for each defendant, and the lawyers needed time to submit sentencing memoranda. Collectively, I had almost one thousand pages to read to prepare for the sentences. In addition, there were a few letters I received from the defendants' friends and relatives. And I received many from Marjorie. In them she poured her heart out for Peter and begged me to go easy on him. They were highly personal. She recounted many intimate details about their loving relationship.

I sentenced Ciccone and Cassarino to 150 and 135 months, respectively. The Lump got 57 months; another defendant named Brancato got 36; Peter's brother, Richard G. Gotti, was sentenced to 33 months; and his nephew, Richard V. Gotti, got 12 months and a day. There was a reason for giving Richard V. the extra day; it would allow him to qualify for the 15 percent good-time credit, meaning he could be out of jail after about 10 months.

I began Peter's sentencing proceeding on Friday, March 26, 2004, almost exactly a year after he had been convicted. I started by identifying all of the papers that I had in my sentencing file—as was my responsibility. I made sure that the lawyers had received the PSR and each other's written submissions. I then told them that I had received many letters from Marjorie Alexander. Because they were sent in confidence, and not part of the public record, I did not disclose their contents—other than to say they were basically supportive and "really don't deal with sentencing issues." However, I would let the lawyers see them if they wanted to. None of the lawyers took me up on the offer, but Andrew Genser—who was handling the sentencing for the government—said that he would just like to make copies of them for the government's file.

I listened to the lawyers' lengthy arguments that day and started to make some of the guidelines calculations. I stopped short of delivering the actual sentence and set it down for a few weeks later. I needed some time to reflect on a number of legal issues that the lawyers had raised but did rule that I believed Peter was indeed the acting boss of the Gambino crime family. Because of that, I said that he might be facing up to fifteen years of jail, although my final decision would not be rendered until the adjourned date.

Marjorie, who showed up every day of the two-month trial, fled the courtroom in tears.

Late that afternoon, my clerk, Mike Innelli, told me that a reporter from the *Daily News* had asked him whether the press could see Marjorie's letters. Since I considered them confidential, I said that they would not be released. On Monday, Mike told me that Genser had asked for copies of the letters. He made the copies and sent them to Genser's office, but he left a voice message to remind him that the letters were not for public consumption; they were only being furnished pursuant to his request.

On Wednesday night I learned that Marjorie Alexander had committed suicide. She had checked into a Red Roof Inn in Nassau County earlier that day, taken a fistful of antidepressants, and tied a bag around her head. Marjorie left a note in the room apologizing to the hotel maid for any trouble she had caused. She had last been seen on Monday when she had spoken to a *Daily News* reporter about her public declarations of love for Peter Gotti. She had told the reporter, "I took a chance. Life is all about taking chances. Now I am destroyed."

It was the first time in my life when I thought that what I had said might have contributed to someone's decision to commit suicide. Although Peter was facing significant jail time—and Marjorie might have eventually taken her life anyway—I wished I had not said he was facing fifteen years two days before. It did not mean that I would be sentencing him to that many years. I felt devastated.

I thought about Marjorie Alexander some years later after the chief operating officer of one of the world's major public works construction companies was convicted in my court for fraudulently obtaining government construction contracts. His crime was that he did not parcel out some of the subcontracts to minority contractors, as required by the law. The trial lasted for three weeks. The defendant was represented by Gus Newman, who at the age of eighty-four was considered the dean of the New York City criminal defense bar and was still capable of trying a terrific case. Each day the defendant, who was out on bail, came to court on time. He was well dressed and sat attentively at the defense counsel's table while the trial was unfolding. He was hardly the criminal type. He had never had any brushes with the law and was a well-respected leader in the public works construction world. He had been responsible for the development and repairs of major highways and public works projects worth billions, such as the West Side Highway in Manhattan, the Brooklyn–Queens Expressway, and the John F. Kennedy Airport. His wife and his seven-months pregnant daughter came to court each day.

Gus Newman's defense was simply that his client was not in charge of handing out the minority contracts and had no knowledge that the law was not being followed. The jury did not agree. He sat expressionless as the foreperson read the guilty verdict. I had no idea what was going through his mind. But I could tell he was distraught. I thought about Marjorie Alexander and told him that he would not be going to jail now and that he might not be facing much, if any, time.

It didn't matter. Two days later, Gus Newman called to tell me that his client had committed suicide. We were both shocked. Mr. Newman told me that he had lunch with him just a few hours before and had no inkling that he was thinking about taking his life; other than his understandable reaction to the jury's verdict, he had never shown any signs of depression at any time before, during, or after the trial. He left a suicide note. In it he apologized to his wife and pregnant daughter. He recognized that he would never see his grandchild but wrote that he did not believe he had done anything wrong and could not go on living knowing that he had been convicted of a crime.

The next day, Marjorie's suicide was reported in the papers. In addition, the *Post* printed intimate excerpts from her letters that had been given—in confidence—to Genser. They spoke of her personal relationship with Peter during the previous fourteen years, about her broken spirit and her need for antidepressant medication. I was angry. I immediately called Genser's office. He was not there, but his assistant, who had been in court during the sentencing proceeding, answered. He told me that Genser had told him on Monday that he should copy the letters once he received them from the court and give them to the *Post* reporter. I wondered whether Marjorie knew that the *Post* had those letters before she decided to end her life.

In fairness to Genser, I gave him an opportunity to explain what had happened. He apologized. He told me that he honestly had "some misunderstandings about the status of these letters" and that he had put "some naive trust in the promise of the reporter not to publish them unless he first received the court's express approval."

Genser was a very zealous and accomplished lawyer for the government, but he was too cozy with the press. I concluded, however, that he had not acted maliciously and was satisfied that he was truly contrite. I used the occasion to write an opinion about when, if at all, judges should make sentencing letters public. My research disclosed that there was very little law on the subject. Balancing the competing interests of the public's general common-law right to have access to court documents with the private rights of confidential letter-writers, I set down a series of guidelines that I would abide by in the future. Basically, the lawyers could still look at the letters—in confidence—and I would only make specific reference to them during the sentencing proceeding if I believed they would have a significant bearing on the sentence. The one exception was that I would disclose any letters received from public officials seeking to use their office to influence the sentence.

On April 15, 2004, I sentenced Peter Gotti to 112 months—a little more than nine years—and wondered whether that might have made a difference for Marjorie since it was much less than the fifteen years I had mentioned before. The guidelines range, which I had to first calculate, came out to be 108 to 135 months. It was complicated stuff. Each of the many racketeering acts that the jury had found to be committed by the Gambinos—and for which Peter was accountable under RICO—carried specific guidelines points and had to be separately considered. As I was going through this tedious process, I looked out at the puzzled spectators in the packed courtroom, some of whom were law students, and felt the need to speak to them about the guidelines:

> There are courses at law schools now devoting a whole year just to sentencing guideline calculations. I know my colleague Judge Gleeson teaches such a course at NYU and it requires a whole year to explain the sentencing guidelines to the law students. I think you probably have some better appreciation of what that world is all about having sat patiently throughout these proceedings. One wonders whether or not they are part of a science class making complex calculations, mathematical calculations, dividing the atom, or whether this is really sentencing that we're talking about.

I find the guidelines to be useful as a guide. I sort of look literally at the word "guideline" and then I try to look to see whether they are creating distortions, and, if so, what mechanisms we have within the law to make sensible adjustments. But it is a challenge to every judge to have to deal with what has become this massive material that we have to master reflected in this big book and all the decisions that emanate from the courts. It is a daunting task, obviously, but one which, of course, we are obliged to attend to.

Gotti's outstanding lawyer then argued that I should downwardly depart from the low end of the guidelines range and sentence his client to no more than four years. Shargel believed that downward departures were indicated under the guidelines, as they then existed—they had yet to become advisory since *Booker* was not then on the books—for a number of reasons: He had been wrongly locked up in solitary confinement for three months; when he was finally let out, he was housed on a floor with inmates who were suffering from serious psychosis; and he had a host of serious medical issues. In that latter regard, Shargel ticked off several health problems, including blindness in one eye, irregular heartbeat, rheumatoid arthritis, gout, sciatica, and emphysema, concluding, "Mr. Gotti is not a well man. He is not your average sixty-five-year-old person. He is in poor health. His life expectancy from all these diseases from which he suffers is diminished by years."

Shargel also pointed out that the only real crime his client was found guilty of was money laundering, which would have carried a fifteen- to twenty-one-month sentence according to the guidelines. He was right about that, but the jury also convicted him of the RICO counts, meaning that it found he was part of a criminal enterprise—namely the Gambino crime family—and had committed at least two crimes, such as money laundering, within a ten-year span as part of the activities of that enterprise. Receiving monies from the activities of the enterprise qualified as money laundering. This was, therefore, a textbook example of what Congress had intended when it enacted

RICO, that being a member of a criminal enterprise would make you responsible for all the foreseeable criminal acts of the enterprise. If not for RICO, Gotti would only be guilty of money laundering and would only be facing a year or two in jail.

Finally, Shargel argued that even though his client might have been the acting boss of the Gambinos, because "there was no one else to put there," he was essentially a figurehead. As he exclaimed, in wrapping up his arguments: "I don't know there's anyone who knows Peter Gotti that thinks he was making any important decisions of any kind."

Shargel's arguments resonated with me, and the sentence I imposed was just slightly higher than the low end of the guidelines range. I had observed his client throughout the lengthy trial, and although I didn't think a downward departure was indicated, I had listened to tons of tapes about the Gambino's lifestyle and criminal misdeeds and Peter Gotti struck me as a relatively passive and benign personality—hardly out of the Godfather mold. But, nonetheless, I told Shargel that "Mr. Gotti had choices. He could have said no, I don't want to be acting boss or have anything to do with the Gambino family or receive kick-ups or however it is characterized. He made a choice to be part of the family."

All of the guilty verdicts were upheld on appeal. It marked the end of one of the most difficult and lengthy trials I ever had. It was not, however, the end for Peter. He was subsequently indicted and convicted in the Southern District of New York for plotting to kill Sammy the Bull for ratting out his brother. In a secretly recorded conversation in May 1997, while John Gotti was rotting in prison, he told Peter that not a day went by when he did not dream of chopping Salvatore Gravano and other turncoats "in little pieces." At Peter's second trial, a Gambino associate testified that in 1999 he learned that Gravano was living in Phoenix and went there on orders from Peter to kill him. The Bull, however, was not there. Nonetheless, Judge Casey sentenced Peter to twenty-five more years for his efforts. Like the Teflon Don, he, too, will die in jail. Sammy the Bull, however, lives on.

It was all written in the cards, befitting the fate of those who joined the Mafia. Cassarino had summed it up during one of the intercepted tapes: "That's life. That's the life we chose."

It may not have come as a big surprise—given the life that Peter Gotti and his fellow Gambinos chose—that they would wind up in jail someday, but it must have come as quite a surprise to the leader of the New York State Senate—given the entirely different life that he chose—that he would suffer the same fate.

6

Public Officials

Pedro Espada Jr.

The Crime

On a cold Tuesday in December 2010, New York State attorney general and governor-elect Andrew Cuomo announced that Pedro Espada Jr., the majority leader of the New York State Senate, had been federally indicted for what Cuomo called "one of the more outrageous abuses of public office that I have ever seen." Espada immediately called it a political "witch hunt," and the press jumped all over it.

The "outrageous" abuse of public office entailed allegations that the fifty-seven-year-old Espada and his thirty-seven-year-old son, Pedro Gautier (who was also indicted), embezzled more than $500,000 from Soundview Health Care Center, a federally funded not-for-profit health care clinic, which Espada founded more than thirty years ago in an impoverished area of the Bronx. Cuomo decried that "there was no doubt" Espada was "looting" Soundview "for a lavish lifestyle" since, according to the indictment, Espada charged his health care clinic, from 2005 to 2009, for such things as $110,000 for meals in posh restaurants, including $20,482 at his favorite sushi place near his home; a down payment on a $125,000 Bentley; $14,000 in tickets for sports and shows; and "pony rides and a petting zoo at a family birthday party."

It would be my first high-profile official corruption trial. When I read the indictment, I did not dismiss the charges as inconsequential; indeed, if Espada were convicted, I would not hesitate to send him to jail, but I thought that Cuomo's characterization of the charges as one of the more outrageous abuses of public office he had ever seen was somewhat hyperbolic since, unlike many other Albany politicians who had recently been convicted, none of the charges against Espada had anything to do with his performance as a legislator. I thought, therefore, that there might be some legitimacy to Espada's political "witch-hunt" claim.

Indeed, I learned that, within days of his election in 2008 to his second stint in the Senate, Espada had threatened his own Democratic majority: He demanded a leadership position for what he said was a needed Latino voice, or he would join the Republicans and end the Democrats' first majority in a half century. Naturally, this did not sit well with the Democratic establishment, especially when Espada carried out the threat in June 2009 in exchange for becoming Senate president. To lure him back, the Democrats had to make him the majority leader.

It must have stuck in their craw. Ironically, as reported in the *Wall Street Journal* on December 17, 2010, just two days after Cuomo announced the indictment, prosecutors acknowledged that "[t]he investigation into Soundview didn't get under way until the spring of 2009"—just about the time Espada made his deal with the Republicans. A senior Cuomo official, who asked not to be identified, stated that "[b]y the time Attorney General Cuomo assumed office in 2007, there was no active investigation and no indicators of any wrongdoing." Moreover, in 2008 and 2009, the state had awarded Soundview a federal capital grant worth $3 million and a federal stimulus grant of $255,000.

Espada possessed a shrewd political sense, and in his bold suits of gold pinstripes in a place long dominated by white men in dark suits, the multilingual Espada, as the first Latino majority leader of the New York State Senate, was a dominant, charismatic figure.

In his typical bravura style, Espada issued a year-end majority-leader report hours before his indictment became public, expounding on the importance of state grants for nonprofit agencies and taking credit for reforms in the Senate to make lawmakers accountable. Immediately after his indictment, he was stripped of his leadership. Months later he would lose his primary for reelection, and the Republicans would take back control of the Senate in the general election.

Taking the high road, Cuomo concluded his remarks after announcing Espada's indictment by lamenting that "there's a culture in Albany that has been too tolerant of legal violations and ethical absences." He added: "We're sending a message today. . . . The days when Albany politicians can victimize taxpayers are over."

Later that day, Espada's lawyer, Susan Necheles, fought back, issuing the following press release: "Thirty years ago Senator Espada founded the Soundview Health Care Center. Soundview has provided high-quality health care to thousands of families, children, and senior citizens in the Bronx. Today is a sad day for Soundview and a sad day for the Espada family. Senator Espada and his son deny any wrongdoing and we intend to fight the charges in court."

The nursing home that I had represented, as a neophyte lawyer, was an important client and the fees I received for doing its legal work went a long way to supporting my wife and two young children while I was struggling to build a practice as a solo practitioner in the middle of suburban Long Island, sixty miles away from the bright Broadway lights where I assumed the lawyers in the big city were making big bucks.

I didn't much relish what I had to do, but it was a legitimate client who was in constant need of legal representation to defend against a barrage of health care violations leveled against the nursing home and its owner by the New York State Department of Health.

While the owner of the facility was never accused of embezzling his health care facility's funds, he was not averse to sacrificing the best interests of his patients to deliver the best health care by cutting corners, if he could get away with it. I guess my job was to help him do that. I'm pretty sure I never crossed the ethical divide in defending him, but if I hadn't needed the money at that time, I probably would not have represented him.

I thought about this while I was reading the Espada indictment and wondered if it might subconsciously affect my judicial responsibility to give the defendants a fair trial.

The trial began in the middle of April 2012, a year and a half after the federal indictment. During that time, the Espadas were at liberty. Bail was set by Magistrate Judge Steven Gold at a $750,000 unsecured bond signed by Espada's wife. No other security was required, but the Espadas had to periodically report to the pretrial services office and comply with a number of rudimentary pretrial release requirements. They did so, without incident.

During that period, I conducted numerous pretrial conferences to address several pretrial motions by the parties and allowed them sufficient time to prepare for the trial.

The courtroom was packed the day the trial began. The press was out in force. I picked the requisite twelve jurors plus a handful of alternates during the morning and started the trial in the afternoon with opening statements from the lawyers. Since the government—as always—had the burden of proving that the defendants were guilty, it went first. The government's prosecution team consisted of three young, fiery assistant U.S. attorneys, Todd Kaminsky, Roger Burlingame, and Carolyn Pokorny, who gave the opening statement.

I've had the pleasure of watching Carolyn Pokorny try a number of cases before me. She remains one of my favorites: articulate and respectful, with a winning personality. But she is also a fierce advocate. In dramatic fashion, her opening remarks went right for the jugular:

> The defendants, Pedro Espada Jr., that man (pointing), and his son, Pedro Gautier Espada, that man (pointing), stole more than half a million dollars from a public charity. They stole that

money so they could spend it on themselves and their families and then they lied to cover the whole thing up.

Now, Pedro Espada and his son Gautier were in charge of this public charity. The charity was a group of medical clinics in the Bronx that served low-income and underprivileged people. These medical clinics received millions of dollars in federal grants and taxpayer money. It was all supposed to go for a good cause.

The Espadas betrayed that trust. They did it because they were greedy. They did it because they were powerful and they did it because they thought they were going to get away with it.

During a five-year spending spree, Espada spent sixty grand on sushi and lobster. The two of them together spent thousands and thousands of the charity's money on scholarship. They called it scholarship. It was really just sending their kids to school, private school, and tutoring for their own family with money that was supposed to go to the sick and the needy.

It paid for their beach vacations, thousands and thousands and thousands of dollars in flowers, spa treatment, family parties, and luxury cars.

And this wasn't just a fraud on the charity. It was also a fraud on the Internal Revenue Service and on the taxpayers, because the defendants lied to their accountants. They lied to their own accountants and they lied to the IRS.

They tried to make it seem like when they were spending all of the charity's money, that it was on legitimate business expenses. It wasn't. They were spending it on themselves and their family and that's what this case is about.

These two men, they have lied, they have cheated, they have stolen and they have betrayed the public's trust and I'm going to go through with you what the government is going to prove to you beyond a reasonable doubt.

She then laid out, with particularity, the government's case. Of course, it would be up to the jury to decide, after listening to all the witnesses and reviewing all the documentary exhibits, whether the government had proven the defendants' guilt.

After she finished, it was the defendants' lawyers turn. Espada was represented by another gifted attorney, Susan Necheles. She cautioned the jurors not to jump to any conclusions until all the evidence was in, and that "[u]nder our constitutional system, the government, when they charge someone with a crime, must prove that person guilty beyond a reasonable doubt." She then argued that the Espadas had done nothing wrong and harped on the fact that it is not a crime to make too much money from a charity:

> If it were a crime to get paid too much money, half of Wall Street would be in jail. They are not. In America, you are allowed to make money, and you are even allowed to make it from a charity.
>
> So when the government talks about "Oh, the Espadas made a lot of money, oh, my gosh," it's not a crime.
>
> We will get later to the facts of what exactly happened here. We will get to that during the trial. But remember this. Keep your eye on the ball. Don't let smears about what kind of things they were spending money on, things that are attempts to divert your attention. Don't let them divert your attention.

Espada's son was represented by Russell Gioiella, another skilled lawyer. He followed Necheles's opening remarks with a low-key approach, portraying his client as an innocent dupe under his father's control.

On May 14, 2012, about six weeks after the trial began, the jury returned a partial verdict after deliberating for eleven days. Eight counts had been submitted to the jury. Four dealt with various embezzlements from 2005 through 2008; the others entailed other alleged misdeeds by the Espadas in the management of Soundview's affairs. The jury unanimously found Pedro Espada Jr. guilty of the embezzlements but could not reach a unanimous verdict on the other counts.

The jurors apparently felt sympathetic to Espada's son since they could not reach a verdict on any of the other counts against him.

The embezzlement counts amounted to a little more than $500,000—$70,000 during 2005; $145,000 during 2006; $160,000 during 2007; and $164,000 during 2008. I accepted the partial verdict. I was satisfied that after eleven days of contentious deliberations the jury was hopelessly deadlocked on the other counts and, accordingly, declared a mistrial on those counts. This meant that the government could, if it wished, retry the Espadas on those counts. I gave them three weeks to decide. If the government chose not to retry the Espadas, I would then dismiss those counts and sentence Pedro Espada Jr. on the four convicted counts of embezzlement.

The next day, the *Wall Street Journal* reported that it had spoken to some of the jurors afterward about the deliberations. Unless there was some extraordinary reason to do so, I would never do that, but the press was pretty much free to do as it pleased.

"There were a lot of emotions in there," one male juror said of the jury room. "You had some jurors there [deliberating] on an emotional basis but logic prevailed." He further told the press that some jurors believed the government had a "vendetta" against the senior Espada and simply convincing them to study the reams of evidence against him took up much of the jurors' time.

Another juror told the newspaper that one juror announced within ten minutes after deliberations commenced that she felt Pedro Espada "was innocent, innocent, innocent, and I will not change my mind." She said this juror was joined by two others, who never stated their reasons, and none of the three ever budged: "That's what we were up against for two weeks. It became very frustrating." Nor apparently did the other jurors budge since she also reported that "[f]rom day one it was nine to three" in favor of a guilty verdict.

This juror also told the press that it was only after the judge had told the jury that it could render a partial verdict, in response to one of the many notes the jury had sent to the judge, that the three dissenters "flip-flopped" on the embezzlement counts, although they remained resolute on the others.

Right after the guilty verdicts were announced, Governor Cuomo released a statement responding to Espada's relentless "witch-hunt" accusations: "Mr. Espada has made many accusations and comments about me since my actions began. Today, the jury spoke loud and clear, making Mr. Espada a convicted felon."

While deciding whether to retry the Espadas on the hung counts, the government brought additional charges against them, including charging the senior Espada with failure to report his ill-gotten gains on his 2005 to 2009 tax returns—something that I imagine no criminal would ever be inclined to do. And his son was also charged with income tax evasion for 2010, as well as a new theft conspiracy count.

Whether or not it was an intentional ploy, it resulted in a joint agreement by the Espadas to enter guilty pleas before me to avoid yet another trial, in exchange for the dismissal of all the outstanding charges in both proceedings. Thus, on October 12, 2012, Espada admitted—in satisfaction of all the tax counts—that for the 2005 tax year he knew that his income was "in excess" of the amount of the $297,630 that he reported. Thus, he did not report, as the jury had found, that he had stolen $70,000 from Soundview that year. And Pedro Gautier pleaded guilty to both of his new charges.

The upshot of it all was that I would be sentencing Espada for the four counts of theft and the new tax count, and his son for the two new charges. As part of their plea agreements, Espada agreed to waive his right to appeal if I sentenced him to eighty-four months or below, and his son waived his appellate rights if his sentence would be twenty-four months or less.

The plea agreements estimated a sentencing guidelines range of seventy to eighty-four for father and a twenty-four-month term of imprisonment for son. The twenty-four months was the statutory maximum for Pedro Gautier, but I was not bound by the estimated range for the more culpable father; under the law, I could impose a sentence up to forty years for Espada.

A number of months passed before I set June 14, 2013, as Espada's sentencing date; I would separately sentence his son the following week. This gave the probation department sufficient time to prepare the presentence report. Furthermore, Espada had changed counsel and his new lawyer, Angelo Cruz, needed time to get up to speed. I allowed the Espadas to remain at liberty during this interregnum since they had faithfully complied with all their pretrial requirements.

I had a general feel for what the appropriate sentences might be but little did I know what awaited me.

The Punishment

From the moment Cuomo had branded Espada's alleged misconduct as "[o]ne of the most outrageous abuses of public office [he] had ever seen," the press jumped on the bandwagon and demonized him as if he were public enemy number one. It echoed the future governor's rhetoric that he was "the prime example of government corruption." The *New York Post* called him "the despicably amoral love-child of Al Capone and Kim Kardashian"; the Albany *Times Union* commented that "Mr. Espada just might qualify as the biggest scoundrel to yet emerge from a state government, particularly a state Legislature, that seems to be a magnet for people of such unseemly character." The *Daily News* reported that he used his not-for-profit health care center "as a personal piggy bank to live high on the hog." The Associated Press stated that Espada had been "at the center of two of the most tumultuous years the two-century-old New York Senate has ever seen."

But Espada came from the school of hard knocks and fought his way up from poverty in the Bronx projects to become a hero in the Latino community. He was a gut fighter and was not going to take the slings and arrows lying down. Each day during the trial, he appeared at press conferences at the entrance to the courthouse, vilifying Cuomo for conducting "this witch hunt" and accusing the prosecution of being in his political pocket. At one point the prosecutors asked me to issue a gag order, but I did not do it, explaining that "I think he's entitled to have all the press conferences he wants. My job is to make sure the jury doesn't hear about it." I had to balance Espada's First Amendment right to freedom of speech with the need to keep the jury focused on the evidence without being influenced by what the press was reporting or what Espada was saying.

Easier said than done. Each day I admonished the jurors not to read or listen to what the press was reporting about the trial or to check it out on the Internet. I told them their oath required them to judge the case "solely on the evidence," but in the real world I knew that it was unlikely that the jurors would remain as "pure as Caesar's wife." All I could do was hope for the best. The case was emotionally charged from the outset, and as it turned out during the jurors' heated deliberations, emotions were very much in play.

Not only did Espada conduct his daily press conferences outside the courthouse, hoping to influence the jury through the media, but he also tried to influence the jury while in the courtroom. His wife, Connie, and other supporters would show up dressed in red to ward off the "evil powers" of the government, as he told the press; Connie wore a red shawl and his hulking bodyguard wore a red suit. At one point during the trial, Espada whipped out a rosary, telling reporters later that "it was to combat witchcraft that prosecutors were using to convince jurors to convict him." And during the government's summation, in full view of the jurors, he paged through the Bible, and also appeared to read the controversial book *Black Robes, White Justice: Why Our Legal System Doesn't Work for Blacks*—penned by the infamous late State Supreme Court Justice "Turn 'Em Loose Bruce" Wright—claiming that the legal system is badly skewed against minority defendants.

I wondered what he might conjure up to avoid being sentenced. I soon found out. Just several days before the scheduled sentencing date, Espada, acting as his own lawyer, filed a pro se motion asking for a new trial because of my misconduct during the jurors' deliberations. Astonishingly, he had somehow obtained a sworn affidavit from Juror No. 11, swearing that on the morning of May 14, the jurors had decided they were hopelessly deadlocked, and after I was so advised by the foreman, I "entered the jury room and spoke to all the jurors." The affidavit then recounted:

> Judge Block stated that we should calm down and reach a verdict in this case. He said the government had spent a lot of

money and that he would accept a partial verdict in this case. I am one hundred percent certain that Judge Block was present and that he spoke to all the jurors on the morning of Monday, May 14, 2012. The defendants and the government were not present. About fifteen minutes after Judge Block's talk with the jurors, we took a hand vote and reached a partial verdict on the rents only against Mr. Pedro Espada.

It was pretty serious stuff. Of course it was absurd. If I had actually done that, it would, in my opinion, have constituted obstruction of justice and be an impeachable crime. But I had to deal with it, so on June 6 I held a hearing to address Espada's motion for a new trial based on this affidavit. It happened to be my seventy-ninth birthday.

The night before, I reflected on the fact that the hearing would also mark the beginning of my twentieth year on the bench. Since the Constitution provides that all federal judges are appointed for life, it is up to the judge to decide when it might be appropriate to "hang up the gavel." If I were a New York state judge, I would have been subject to the state's seventy-year-old mandatory retirement law. I believe that all states have such laws and that only federal court judges can serve for life. Perhaps, rather than letting Mother Nature take her toll, I thought that I might end my judicial career with the Espada case.

But I was taken by the fact that at the time, the court had five functioning judges in their nineties, led by the venerable Judge Jack Weinstein, who was then ninety-two. I had spoken with Judge Weinstein about how we should know "when it might be time to move on." He showed me a letter he had written to Supreme Court Justice Thurgood Marshall asking him that question when Judge Weinstein, who had then been on the bench for a quarter century, had reached the state's mandatory seventy-year-old retirement age. After he had graduated from Columbia Law School, Judge Weinstein had worked under Marshall's tutelage for the NAACP Legal Defense and Educa-

tional Fund and listened to the future first African American Supreme Court Justice argue Brown v. Board of Education *in 1952. Judge Weinstein's name is forever memorialized as one of the signatories to the Brown Supreme Court brief.*

Judge Weinstein's letter to Justice Marshall hangs on the wall of Judge Weinstein's office, together with the justice's reply on July 16, 1992. At that time, Justice Marshall had been retired from the high court for the past several months. In the reply, he praised Judge Weinstein's brilliant achievements and told him that he surely could proudly retire at that time. But he shared with him these personal thoughts:

> You know that this problem of whether or not to retire or whether to take senior status is absolutely a personal one and there is no help anybody can give. I have for myself narrowed it down to the doctor, my wife, and me. Together we went over all of the conditions year after year and eventually the doctor persuaded us that it was time to retire and I retired.

Thurgood Marshall died six months later. Judge Weinstein is still going strong, with a full caseload, at the ripe-old age of ninety-seven. Last year, the Court's Ceremonial Courtroom was named in his honor on the occasion of his fiftieth year on the bench.

When the founding fathers, in their zeal to create a totally independent federal judiciary, decided that the judges should be given life tenure, dementia and Alzheimer's was not a known concern since judges invariably never lived into their eighties, let alone nineties. But even though we can now linger on into real old age, the judges of my court are mindful that we have a responsibility to ensure the public does not suffer if one of us starts to lose it. It's an informal process. Help is offered for difficult cases; conversations take place with trusted colleagues. It's sensitive stuff but is largely effective.

As for my inner soul-searching, on the eve of having to manage Espada's frontal challenge against my judicial integrity and competency to properly discharge my oath of office, my doctor and wife assured me that I could still effectively function and the time had not yet come to leave the bench. Happily, I have continued to get that assurance to the present.

The first thing that happened at the hearing was an application by Espada's lawyer, Mr. Cruz, to be relieved. He had advised Espada against making his motion; his client did not take his advice, and he believed there was a breakdown in their relationship that was "irrevocable." I explained to him that he had submitted an excellent set of sentencing papers and that on the eve of sentencing I would not let Espada get another lawyer. It would just serve to further delay judgment day for some indeterminate period of time.

I then addressed Espada's motion. I explained that I was at home when I received an email from my courtroom clerk stating that the jury had reached a partial verdict. I then spoke with my clerk and told him to notify counsel that I was on my way. The court trial record reflects that I took the bench at 12:05 p.m. and that the jury returned to the courtroom two minutes later, at which time the foreperson publicly announced the partial verdict. Thus, I stated that at the time when I supposedly entered the jury room that morning, as Juror No. 11 had stated, "I was not even in the courthouse."

Consequently, I asked Espada if he wished to withdraw his motion. If not, I might have to send the matter to another judge, because unless there was clear documentary evidence that I was not in the courthouse, my credibility would be at issue; I would have to be 100 percent circumspect and not be my own judge and jury. But Espada stood firm and asked, through his lawyer, if he could have until the following Monday, June 10, to decide. Instead of withdrawing his absurd motion, he sent me a letter on that date asking for permission to interview all the other jurors "to ascertain all relevant facts and evidence concerning [my] ex parte communication with the deliberating jury." He referenced the affidavit submitted by Juror No. 11 as providing "a solid foundation for this request." Accordingly, he requested the scheduled sentencing date be adjourned and that a hearing be held "so that all the relevant evidence and facts can be established."

As good fortune would have it, I was able to obtain documentary evidence after the court proceedings, which allowed me to reject Espada's shenanigans and not impose the burden on another judge to deal with Espada's efforts to avoid judgment day.

On the scheduled sentencing date, four days later, just before I started the sentencing proceeding, I formally disposed of Espada's motion. I marked as Exhibit A an email that my clerk had sent to me advising that all the jurors had begun their deliberations that morning at 10:08 a.m.; a note from my clerk to the chief clerk of the court and the lawyers at 10:45 a.m. that "we will be taking a partial verdict in the Espada case today at 11:30 a.m.," which I marked as Exhibit B; an email that one of the government's lawyers sent to her office at 10:50 a.m., marked Exhibit C, stating: "Don't rush over. Judge won't be here until 11:30. Partial verdict will be given then;" and finally two killer exhibits that doomed Espada's fate.

The first, marked Exhibit D, included phone records showing that at 10:37 a.m. I received a call from my law clerk on my chamber's telephone to my home telephone in Manhattan just two minutes after I received my clerk's email advising that a verdict had been reached. The second, which I marked Exhibit E, was a surprise. It showed that at precisely 11:48.56 a.m., I had swiped my access card to allow my car to get into the court's garage, and I entered the judicial elevator from the garage at 11:51.58 a.m. and reached my chambers two minutes later. I learned, therefore, that Big Brother had records of just about every move I made in the courthouse. I assumed there was at least one exception and quipped that "I'm glad there's no access card in the men's room here."

Accordingly, I concluded that "I'm comfortable we have documentary evidence here that I was not in the building when Juror No. 11 swore under penalties of perjury 100 percent that I was here. So I don't have to burden any of my colleagues with referring this matter, since my credibility is not at all at issue here." I then stated that I was referring the matter of the perjured affidavit to the U.S. Attorney's Office so it could consider whether to bring criminal charges against the lying juror, and, finally, turned to sentencing Espada.

I had previously told Espada's lawyer when the frivolous motion for a new trial was first discussed the week before that I would not hold it against his client at the sentencing:

> He is going to be sentenced based upon sentencing factors, based upon your submissions, based upon everything that's happened here. I assure you it's a matter of professional pride on my part that I will not let the filing of that motion influence the sentence in one iota. He is entitled to fight for his life. He is entitled to do what he thinks appropriate. Maybe it is misguided, maybe it's not the wisest thing to do, but I am not going to let that influence my sentencing decision. It would be improper for me to do that.

It looked good in print, but before I began the sentencing hearing to determine how much jail time I would give Espada, I wondered if I could truly shake the assault on my professional integrity from my subconscious. To guard against that possibility, I had consulted with a few of my colleagues.

In a run-of-the-mill case, I relied on my years of experience in coming to an appropriate sentence. Of course, each case is important and there is no such thing as treating any loss of a person's liberty cavalierly. But I didn't need, for example, to reach out for help on such repetitive cases as drug importations. There was a certain criminal uniformity to them, and I did not think I needed to impose on my colleagues for their advice. But occasionally I had a sentence that puzzled me and I would discuss it with other judges. This was one of those cases. I felt that, given Espada's freewheeling courtroom antics, the heightened press attention, the political ramifications, and Espada's attack against my integrity, I would benefit from the counsel of my colleagues.

I had reached out to two. One had a reputation for being a straight guidelines sentencer, and the other would frequently hand out a below guidelines sentence. We collectively reviewed the presentence report—detailing the crimes of conviction, all relevant conduct, and Espada's personal characteristics. The heavier sentencer thought seven years was the right number; the other thought six was more appropriate. I thought they both were on the high side, but their opinions weighed on my mind during the sentencing proceeding.

I thought about one more thing. The weekend before, I had dinner with Judith Sheindlin, better known as Judge Judy, at her magnificent estate in Greenwich, Connecticut. She had been one of my clients when she was the supervising judge of the New York City Family Court before she became Judge Judy; I had successfully represented the family court judges in a pay parity litigation against the state so that they would receive the same compensation as their higher paid colleagues in neighboring Nassau and Suffolk Counties. She had followed the Espada trial and knew that the sentence was coming up in a few days. We didn't talk about the sentence, but she let slip, in her candid, direct style, that if I gave him jail time—which she assumed would be the case—I should not let him walk out of the courthouse and should "remand him right on the spot." I had told her that my usual practice in nonviolent cases was to allow the defendant a few weeks of liberty to get his or her affairs in order.

As is my custom, I started the proceeding by first identifying what I had in my sentencing file. It included the presentence report prepared by the probation department detailing the nature of the crimes and Espada's personal history dating to his early childhood, including many good deeds. It calculated the guideline range at seventy to eighty-seven months. In a separate submission, the probation department recommended a below-guidelines sentence of sixty months, which I was not bound to follow. The PSR explained why it believed a departure was warranted:

> The defendant established Soundview Healthcare Network by himself, which for thirty-one years, serviced a needy population. According to the testimony of multiple witnesses, Soundview provided good medical care for thousands of individuals.

While he ultimately used his role at Soundview to line his own pockets, his creation and operation of an entity that provided public good for many years cannot be ignored. He was also an elected official who provided some civic benefits through his position. His charitable works for the greater good have merit in sentencing, although he ultimately abused his position of trust.

I also identified the underlying plea agreement stemming from the tax fraud indictment, which estimated the same guidelines range of seventy to eighty-seven months of imprisonment.

I had also received extensive memoranda from the lawyers, and many letters of support, as well as a letter from a disgruntled former Soundview employee complaining that Espada never remitted withholdings from his paychecks to the IRS. Espada's lawyer pleaded for a non-incarceratory sentence; the government thought a guidelines sentence was warranted.

There was one matter I had to attend to before dealing with incarceration. I entered a forfeiture order proposed by the government, which would require Espada to cough up $368,088 as the fruits of his crime. I then made the requisite guidelines calculation. I agreed that the PSR and plea agreement calculations were correct, and then invited counsel to speak:

> So now we come to the point in the proceeding where we have to determine the appropriate punishment for Mr. Espada. And I believe strongly in having interactive dynamics when it comes to sentencing. I share with you some of my concerns on both sides, to invite your thoughts. I come in here with a general idea of where I'm going. I always hold back in . . . making my final determination until I hear fully from counsel, and Mr. Espada has a right to speak.

Before the government spoke, I shared with the prosecutors "where my mind-set is," noting Espada's "laudatory past good deeds," and that "Soundview was obviously investigated many times by the health authorities" without "any evidence that there was anything wrong with the health care that was provided." I commented that that impressed me "because although [Espada] obviously has acted in this palpable way and he's going to be punished for it, the people in the community were apparently given good health care."

AUSA Kaminsky spoke for the government. He urged a sentence of eighty-seven months—the high end of the guidelines—because the money Espada appropriated for himself "could have gone to directly benefit poor people and help them get health care." But when I questioned him as to whether "another four hundred, five hundred, six hundred thousand dollars over that [four]-year period" would have really made a major difference in the health care that was provided, given that Soundview furnished medical care to "twenty-one thousand people that would not have gotten it otherwise," Kaminsky backed off, stating that "a sentence closer to Probation's number would of course also be appropriate." He nonetheless hewed to his position that the high end of the guidelines was more appropriate, as reflected in the following interactive colloquy we engaged in.

> **KAMINSKY:** But when you look for what mitigating factors might exist, let me give you some examples: was this a one-time offense or something the defendant [did] in isolated instances? Of course, it was not. Over and over, he made thousands of decisions full of criminal intent.
>
> Was this money that was made to save a family member, to pay a crushing debt, to help a relative in a foreign country? It was not. This is money that went to sushi and lobster dinners, to fancy vacations, fancy parties.
>
> **THE COURT:** You're really loading it up on him, you know, just putting out everything he ate.
>
> One of the things that also impressed me, just to continue on our interactive dialogue, is that some of these gifts were to Connie, his wife, and family. He seems to have really a supportive family. I didn't see any evidence of any mistresses. There isn't a politician in Albany who doesn't have a mistress, but who knows?
>
> But he seems to be a real solid family man, and while I don't condone the fact that he was using Soundview for gift certificates

and vacations to Puerto Rico, they were all for Connie. I mean, it's a nice kind of love affair. Do you place any stock in that?

KAMINSKY: I don't, Your Honor. I think a dollar that could have gone to help someone get proper dentures, whether it goes to someone's wife or someone's mistress is a dollar that's misappropriated. And all of us would love to provide ponies at our children's parties and take fancy vacations at the nicest hotels, but we have—

THE COURT: I agree with that, but do you think that under 3553(a), I should consider the nature of his family relationships? He has three children, one of whom is going to be sentenced next week, but the other two apparently are hardworking kids. The family seems to be intact.

He talks about having to sleep in the subways while he was in high school, and he turns out to be a solid family man. Do you think it's really worthy of consideration under 3553(a)(1)?

KAMINSKY: Yes, Your Honor. That's something you can consider or even should consider, but it's in the government's opinion, dwarfed by the egregious criminal conduct here, and the defendant's clear belief that he's entitled to do what he did.

Kaminsky further focused on the fact that even though Espada acknowledged his criminal conduct in his plea agreement, he did a "180 degree turn since then," reflecting a total lack of remorse. According to Kaminsky, Espada "stood about a hundred yards from here on the street last week and said, 'I've never stolen a dime in my life and I've never cheated on a tax return.'" And, not surprisingly, Kaminsky added to the mix Espada's phony claim that I had tampered with the jurors during their deliberations, wrapping up his remarks in dramatic fashion:

It's clear that Mr. Espada believes that he is infallible and that he did absolutely nothing wrong, and as we're sitting here today, in light of such a despicable offense and yet zero remorse, I think that's something that should dwarf many of the considerations that would ordinarily favor a defendant. I think it's absolutely—for lack of a better word, Your Honor, it's just simply appalling.

It was Espada's counsel's turn. I questioned him about the PSR reporting that subsequent to his conviction he accepted payment of $144,000 from Soundview's board of directors for monies allegedly properly owed to him that could have gone to other creditors. Mr. Cruz explained that Espada was broke and was legally entitled to that money. He then faulted the government for Soundview's financial problems because it reneged on a $2 million grant it had authorized and focused on Espada's good deeds. We engaged in the following colloquy:

> **CRUZ:** In addition to what we have already presented in our sentencing memo on behalf of Mr. Espada, I do believe that there are at least a number of things that needs to be emphasized. . . .
>
> You may not like Mr. Espada. You may not like the way he dresses. You may not like the way he talks. You may not like the fact that he comes from the Bronx and pulled himself up.
>
> **THE COURT:** I like the fact that he came from the Bronx and pulled himself up.
>
> **CRUZ:** You may not like the fact that as a senator, he had the audacity to demand a seat at the table and stop the government, if you will, with this supposed coup. You may not like the fact that the media has vilified him as one who consistently always puts his own interest before that of his staff.
>
> **THE COURT:** What's difficult when I write about sentencing . . . is that we all seem to acknowledge this is the toughest part of our job, and one of the reasons why it's tough is because the media has a very real interest in reporting things, and they do report things, and you sort of have to detach yourself a little bit about it and not be influenced by the media and the media's opinions about . . . Mr. Espada. So I try to detach myself from

that and just look at what I have in front of me. I just want to give you that comfort level.

CRUZ: I mean, to his family, he is a loving father. He is a loving father. He is a loving son. To the Soundview community, he remains one who puts them before him. . . .

I'm not going to go over all the many things that he's done, Your Honor. I think you had it when you put that on the record, but I do believe that a noncustodial sentence is appropriate and sufficient to meet the goals of the sentencing guidelines. . . .

Mr. Espada has been stripped of all the trappings of success. He has been stripped of his money, stripped of his power. He's lost everything, and he needs to grapple with that.

He has been decimated, and his convictions will overshadow the good works that he's done, and that's recognized. Surely, Mr. Espada's career has ended in an instant. He's almost sixty years old now.

He went to see his mother yesterday, not knowing what the outcome was. His mother's elderly. And I can only imagine what he told his mother what he was facing. I know that the Soundview community continues to stand behind him because they remember the many good things that he's done.

His life is not over, Judge. There's still redeeming qualities about him, and a sentence of incarceration I believe is not appropriate. He has been punished enough. To further incarcerate him, I don't believe meets the ends of justice.

He's not lost on the world, Your Honor. His family loves him. His community continues to believe in him. He's going to do many good things. He's charismatic, and—through his own will—he was able to overcome the many adversities that he was confronted with. So although he stands before you today as a convicted felon, I would ask the Court to temper its justice with compassion and not incarcerate him.

It was now Espada's legal right to speak before I rendered my sentence.

Although he accepted responsibility for the tax charge, he would not acknowledge any other criminal wrongdoing. To that extent, Kaminsky was right. He was totally unrepentant. He chose, instead, to extol the virtues of Soundview because it was "the centerpiece of my life's work," and his loyalty to his family. True to his political talents, he was a gifted and articulate speaker. He explained that he started Soundview when he was just twenty-three years old, and it was "a medically underserved and today, remains a medically underserved area." As he elaborated:

> The levels of diabetes are incredible and the cardiovascular disease leads the nation. And in the eighties, when the HIV epidemic hit, it took a while for the world to notice that people of color were disproportionately affected, but it didn't take us a long time because we were pioneers in the efforts to do clinical trials and to deal with that. . . .
>
> Physicians came from throughout the world—literally, throughout the world, idealistic young physicians came because the government paid their way through medical school and they gave back. In fact, Soundview was the medical home not just for patients, but for physicians who came back to give. That is the culture of Soundview, the period in question from '05 to '08 as it relates to me could never and should never define Soundview and its good work.

Espada proudly stated that there were "[t]wenty-five thousand patients, Your Honor, a hundred thousand visits per year, hundreds of jobs and—of quality salaries paid to people," and bemoaned the fact that now Soundview and all its satellite clinics were gone. But, as reflected in the following colloquy between the two of us, he persisted in not accepting responsibility for the crimes of conviction, or even for the bogus jury tampering charge that he had leveled against me.

THE COURT: You accept responsibility for this? I mean, you seem to go both ways. . . . As Mr. Kaminsky said, you're saying one thing in court and then you say something out of court. I have no idea what your sense is in terms of the fact that you've been convicted of these serious crimes.

ESPADA: Your Honor, my son and I came here before Your Honor and we pled guilty. Since that point, Your Honor—

THE COURT: You pled guilty to the tax count. I know that.

ESPADA: But since that point, Your Honor—and you articulated that I had a right to fight for my liberty, and new evidence surfaced, and I filed pro se.

THE COURT: Right.

ESPADA: I am at this point not addressing that issue because it's still something I would like to comment on in a couple of seconds.

THE COURT: You can comment on anything you want.

ESPADA: Okay. But what I'm saying is, Your Honor, Soundview, just for the moment, has been depicted as this piggy bank, as this lifeless subject of theft, when in fact, Soundview—separate from me—was so much more to twenty-five thousand people more than thirty years, that if there be some finality here today to this chapter in my life, let's not end it by describing Soundview as some piggy bank.

It was a medical home and a lifeline to thousands upon thousands of people, and I just beg your indulgence in that area. Set the record straight that what I created when I was a young man was not a piggy bank, but a lifeline to this community that served hundreds of thousands of patients for years.

THE COURT: No, I agree with that. You did use the funds for your own personal purposes. And [from] the records—I listened to the trial—it's overwhelming that you did that.

So anyway, that's what I mean when I talk about using it as your own personal piggy bank. Go ahead. What?

ESPADA: I just wanted to separate, Your Honor—

THE COURT: Right.

ESPADA: —the issue that pertains to me, versus the general description of Soundview, which is totally undeserved.

I am a fifty-nine-year-old man. I've never shied away from any battle or any fight in my life, as the history said. And I stepped in here in this courtroom and accepted responsibility for the tax evasion charge.

THE COURT: Right. But how about the other charges that you were convicted on? You don't have to comment. I'm just giving you the opportunity.

ESPADA: That conviction is an issue in the Rule 33 motion, Your Honor, and I would not like to characterize or comment with respect to that here today.

Espada chose, instead, to once again return to talking about Soundview: "What also happened for thirty years was tremendous quality of care to people who would otherwise be dependent on emergency rooms," and after I told him that sentencing is the "hardest job for a judge," he wrapped up his comments by acknowledging that and talking about his family:

ESPADA: I appreciate Your Honor's sensitivity in that area and it lives on its own, too, in terms of your fairness. But you do as you wish, Your Honor, because that is your job.

But what my job here is to tell you that I have been a lot of things. Right now, mostly, I'm a grandfather of eleven children. And my boys are grown-up men. And I look forward to molding, as I have, my forty-year relationship with my wife and with my family and with my mother who's still alive, and to give back.

There was a statement made about not paying back. I look forward to the opportunity to be employed again. To work, to make amends, and to do what I have to do, mostly, for my family because I know what it is to be a head of household since age fourteen. I don't want those grandchildren to be without their grandfather because I can still provide. I still wish to make amends, to provide, and continue to be supportive of them.

And so if anything, consider the fact that I wish to be available to them as their grandfather and to my wife, as a husband. She did not just receive gifts from me through Soundview. She received a great deal of love and I got it back from her, tenfold, Your Honor.

Thank you very much.

I told Espada that his comments were "[w]ell spoken," addressed some collateral sentencing issues regarding restitution, including a requirement that he repay the IRS $118,000, and announced that I would render the sentence after a short recess.

When I told Espada that sentencing was a judge's "hardest job," I also commented that "I've had nothing but sleepless nights" because "I have to be like God and pick a number out here." During the recess, I sat alone in my private robing room behind the courtroom and painstakingly ruminated about what that number should be. A number of thoughts flashed through my mind: Should I take into consideration the attack against my judicial integrity? Was there an element of truth to Espada's claim that the Democratic establishment, led by the future governor, was "out to get him"? Indeed, would the investigation into his inappropriate American Express charges ever have taken place if not for Espada's brazen political gamesmanship? How should I balance his misuse of Soundview's funds during the five-year period when his American Express account was being gone over with a fine-tooth comb, with the importance of the health care Soundview provided to a challenged minority community for decades? How should I account for the fact that his misdeeds did not involve the abuse of his political office, unlike many Albany legislators who had been convicted in the recent past? How much weight should I give to the fact that he had a loving family and an apparent lasting love affair with his wife, who was the principal beneficiary of his misdeeds? How much weight should I give to his failure to take any responsibility for the crimes of conviction? Should I consider his behavior in the courtroom or his contentious behavior outside the courtroom as negatively reflective of his character? And last, given these imponderables, should I err on the side of leniency? For surely, if I did, I might not have more sleepless nights.

Although I often do not do so, I decided here to go along with the recommendation of the probation department and sentenced Espada to five years. It was ten months below the lowest end of the advisory guidelines, but I gave significant credit to the good deeds he had "done in the community" and "the good deeds of [his] past life."

There was one more matter that had to be attended to. Should I put Espada in jail now—as Judge Judy would—or give him some time to get his affairs in order and self-surrender? As I told my former client, that was my usual practice in nonviolent cases.

Although I do not think I was influenced by her gratuitous opinion, I did put him in jail on the spot. I reasoned that, given the grief he caused Juror No. 11, I did not want to give him any opportunity to impose himself on any other juror.

The government decided not to prosecute that beleaguered juror after he acknowledged that he was mistaken.

The following week I sentenced Espada's son to six months. He was obviously under the control of his father, and, unlike his father, he had acknowledged his relatively minor misdeeds and showed legitimate remorse.

I tried to put the Espada case behind me, but it was not easy. I still had some sleepless nights wondering how all the imponderables in this high-profile case might have been embedded in my subconscious and affected my judgments. On one hand, I thought that five years might have been too severe, but on the other hand I was mindful that one of the goals of sentencing was to "send a message" to other would-be violators of the public trust, and if more than five years would make a difference, perhaps I should have gone along with the government's recommendation of eighty-seven months.

∽

I did a little research. I learned that during the decade prior to Espada's prosecution, eleven members of the New York state legislature had been convicted and sent to jail for using their political office to commit a host of crimes, such as extortion, bribery, mail fraud, and embezzlement. But in my final analysis, I thought that five years was sufficient to send the appropriate message. It was still a significant number of years, and I reasoned that no public official would relish being sentenced to such a lengthy term of imprisonment.

I was wrong. During the five years after Espada was sent to jail, nine more state legislators were imprisoned for abusing their public office. Their crimes included bribery, extortion, fraud, embezzlement, and theft. Shockingly, the most recent convictions entailed extortions by the speaker of the Assembly and the Senate majority leader. Together with the governor, the three of them were often referred to as the "three men in the room," shaping the laws enacted by the state legislature.

Regrettably, two of the governor's trusted aides were also recently convicted of crimes. One was his executive deputy secretary, who was convicted for bribery; the other, the governor's deputy chief of staff when the governor was secretary of HUD, was convicted for theft.

I doubt whether a more severe sentence for Espada would have made a difference. Unfortunately, Albany remains a hotbed of political corruption.

∽

I often think about Todd Kaminsky. As a young assistant U.S. attorney, he was part of the superb team of prosecutors for the government.

Most AUSAs segue into the private sector of the law after putting in a stint at the U.S. Attorney's Office, and pretty soon they are earning big bucks with big law firms representing well-heeled, white-collar criminals. But not Todd. He left the office shortly after the Espada case and successfully ran for the state assembly. He had decided to forgo the lure of the big pay days of private practice to pursue a career of public service.

After the majority leader of the state senate was convicted, his seat became vacant. Defying political odds, Todd was elected to fill it.

During his campaign, Todd was the beneficiary of thousands of robocalls from the famous actor-comedian Mel Brooks, who started his campaign pitch for Todd by saying, "I really am Todd Kaminsky's great-uncle." As fate would have it, one day I was having dinner at Palma, one of my favorite New York City restaurants, when the owner introduced me to the man sitting at the next table. Sure enough it was Mel Brooks. He knew all about the Espada case. I told him that I was the judge and that his great-nephew had done a terrific job. I also told him that we are both in the people business, except that "you have spent your whole career making people laugh, while I have spent mine making them cry." I got a big laugh out of him.

Todd Kaminsky serves the state senate with distinction to this day. I'm very proud of him. Albany certainly needs more like him.

Faced with an embarrassing slew of convictions since his prediction that "[t]he days when Albany politicians can victimize taxpayers are over," the governor has remained unscathed.

7

Collateral Consequences

Chevelle Nesbeth

The Crime

As soon as the word "guilty" rang from the lips of the jury foreperson, she started to cry. She was still crying when she was led from the courtroom many minutes later, propped up by her lawyer.

Chevelle Nesbeth, who months before was a teenager, had just been convicted of attempting to smuggle 602 grams of cocaine into the country. The jury didn't buy her improbable story that she did not know the drugs had been planted in the rails of her two suitcases in Jamaica, where she had been visiting her sick grandparents.

Chevelle was born in Kingston, Jamaica, but when she was thirteen, her mother brought her to the United States. They settled in New Haven, Connecticut, and became citizens. At the time of her conviction, she was a student in good standing at Southern Connecticut State University, studying education. Her dream was to become a school principal. She supported herself as a nail technician at a children's spa, worked as a counselor at a facility that provided services to children in lower-income areas, and during the summers also held seasonal employment as a parks maintenance worker where she was "a youth initiative worker."

Chevelle's mother was "shocked" by her daughter's conviction because it was "completely out of character." She would describe her daughter as an "excellent person, who [was] quiet, nice, caring, and who [was] both very loving and very loved." And to her mother's knowledge, her daughter "never used illegal drugs, consumed alcohol, or required substance abuse treatment."

It was certainly not my first drug importation case. Because JFK Airport is located within its jurisdiction, the Eastern District of New York federal court handles a major number of the country's criminal drug cases. But even though the customs agents do a terrific job in picking up the couriers at the airport, I'm told that they only catch about 10 percent of the smugglers.

As I listened to the evidence unfold, I thought about a number of other drug smuggling cases I had handled over the years and the different bogus stories that the defendants told to escape being convicted. None of them were ever successful, but I had heard them all. However, this was the first one where the drugs were hidden in the rails of suitcases. I've had pregnant women with their children carrying drugs in hidden places, a guy with drugs in his dog's stomach, and a trial with a blind defendant who had liquid cocaine in his knapsack, allegedly put there without his knowledge by someone he could not see. And, of course, there were the desperate swallowers, risking their lives, just like the riveting movie from 2004, Maria Full of Grace. *But I soon realized that none of them fit the razor-clean profile of Chevelle Nesbeth.*

It had been a short trial. It was done and over in just a few days. The government's main witness was the customs agent who punched a hole in the rail of one of the suitcases and discovered the powdery substance. Other government witnesses testified that the powder was indeed cocaine and that it had a street value of "upward of $60,000." The principal piece of documentary evidence was a video clip of the defendant watching as the agent discovered the drugs.

The defendant offered no evidence. She did not have to. She could, as often is the case with a defendant who is obviously guilty, rely upon the obligation of the government to prove guilt beyond a reasonable doubt, and simply argue that the government did not meet that high burden.

In his summation, the prosecutor, AUSA Paul Scotti, correctly told the jurors that there was only one issue for them to decide: "Did she know?" He argued that "the evidence here proves to you that she knew in several important ways." First and foremost, he pointed out that she had admitted to the customs officer that they were her bags, that everything inside them were her clothes, and that she had packed them herself. Next, he called their attention to the video that showed the extendable pull handle on the larger of the two bags "barely came out," suggesting that "[it] was specially altered to fit more cocaine in there." Imploring the jurors to use their "common sense," the prosecutor drove the point home:

> **SCOTTI:** Also, ladies and gentlemen, you know that the defendant had knowledge because of how it was hidden. This wasn't just slipped into the pocket of the bag. These were in the handrails. That is a labor-intensive process, right?
>
> You heard evidence that she went home and she stayed with her family for two weeks. These were her suitcases.
>
> How did that happen? How could somebody get to her bags and fill them with cocaine in the rails? You know that that couldn't happen. It's just the defendant would have to be the most unlucky person in the world, if someone could get to her bags, take the rails apart, fill them up with cocaine, put them back together, without her knowing, and then the handrail of

this one, barely extends? That's not—we already talked about how that's not normal.

After they doctored her bags and altered them, wouldn't she have realized? Wouldn't she have seen that was a problem? No reaction from her in that airport. No problem with extending the rail or pulling on them or doing any of the things that someone who identified that their own bag was not working properly would do, would pull on it, would question it. There was no question from her.

Scotti also pointed out that no one was going to give someone $60,000 worth of drugs who they did not know and trust, and logically argued:

If she didn't know those drugs were in her bag, how was whoever snuck it in there going to get it back from her? Nobody is just giving that to someone who doesn't know and then crossing their fingers and stating, "I hope this gets over there." Then what? Then what do you do? Were they going to steal them from her? Were they going to mug her? How were they going to get the bags back? That's a lot of money.

From watching the jurors, it seemed to me that the prosecutor had put the proverbial nails in the coffin as he succinctly and effectively wrapped up his relatively brief summation:

Those bags could not have been taken from her, taken apart, have cocaine put inside, put back together, with the larger suitcase and the extendible rail clearly, clearly altered, and the defendant just think it was fine and come in here and be none the wiser.

Ladies and gentlemen, the defendant brought $60,000 of cocaine into this country. She knew it. The evidence proves it. I ask that you find her guilty.

It was the defendant's lawyer's turn to sum up. The job of a criminal defense attorney is never easy, especially when it is obvious that the defendant is clearly guilty. Because she did not have sufficient financial resources to hire a private lawyer, the defendant was represented by one of the fine attorneys from the federal defender's office, Amanda David.

This was obviously an open-and-shut case, and I wondered what the defendant's lawyer could possibly say.

She didn't mince words. Right off the bat, Ms. David agreed that "[k]nowledge is absolutely the key issue in this case," and "is the only thing that's really in dispute." She then asked a series of rhetorical questions:

> Where is the evidence? Where is the evidence that Chevelle saw the drugs being placed into the handrails of her bags; that she was told about it; that she was cued in about it; that it was even hinted to her? Where is the evidence of how long she even had these bags before she got to JFK that day?

I suspect the jury must have been as quizzical as I was as the defendant's lawyer spoke these words. She was asking the jury to hold the government accountable because it did not have evidence of the drugs being placed in the handrails by the defendant before she boarded the plane back in Jamaica. It was, of course, absurd, but as the defendant's lawyer, she had to say something.

I have nothing but the greatest respect for the cadre of federal defenders whose job it is to give their assigned clients their best shot and to keep the government's feet to the fire to make sure that the defendant's constitutional rights are not violated. Representing an obviously guilty defendant who is caught red-handed is a tough calling. Most of the time, the lawyers are able to work out a plea agreement but if the defendant wants to go to trial, the lawyer has no choice but to wing it.

Chevelle's lawyer wrapped up her summation by telling the jurors that if they carefully studied the video, they would see the face of an innocent person:

> Think about Chevelle's reaction when the drugs are discovered or even during the secondary inspection. Now, the government wants you to believe that Chevelle has full knowledge that there is cocaine in the handrails of these bags. Yet, she talks to the customs agent. They have a chat, a friendly conversation.
>
> You will hear in government's Exhibit 17A, when he asks her questions about where she lives, about where she is going, about if she works, what her dad does, and she is trying to explain to the customs agent what her father does for a living. And then he suddenly starts tapping the bag; and that's when she says, "Is something wrong?" But before that he has already unzipped the lining of the bag, gotten to the handrails. This should be the moment where the panic sets in. The panic should be setting into Chevelle's face, if she knows there are drugs in there, because it's clear. It would be clear in the mind of someone who knew that they were about to be discovered.
>
> But none of that, none of that is on her face. None of that governs any of her body at all. She stands there, calm, not looking nervous, and only starts to become confused. Then, even after, even after he bangs on the bag, he tells her to repack the bag, which she does, even after all of that, when the bags are taken down and she is waiting to see what's going on, at this point you would think she must know that she has been discovered. Because why else is she still standing there after this man has looked at the handrails so carefully, after he has pounded the place where the drugs are? If she knew they were there.
>
> Let's look at the clip of her after all of this is happening.

I had looked at the clip carefully as it was being shown to the jurors and marveled at how Ms. David could say with a straight face that it showed the face and reaction of an innocent person.

After the summations, I charged the jurors on the law. As for the critical issue of "knowledge," I explained:

> A person acts knowingly if she acts voluntarily and purposefully and not because of a mistake, negligence, or other innocent reason. A person acts intentionally if she acts deliberately and with the specific intent to do something the law forbids. A defendant need not be aware of the specific law or rule that her conduct may be violating. But she must act with the specific intent to do whatever the law proscribes, in this case, import cocaine into the United States.
>
> Although the government must prove that the defendant knew that she was importing cocaine, the government does not have to prove that the defendant knew the exact quantity of the drugs which she is charged with importing. It is enough that the government proves that the defendant knew that she was importing cocaine.
>
> These issues of knowledge and intent require you to make a determination about the defendant's state of mind, something that can rarely be proven directly. A wise and careful consideration of all the circumstances before you may, however, permit you to make a determination as to the defendant's state of mind. Indeed, in your everyday affairs, you are frequently called upon to determine a person's state of mind from his or her words and actions in given circumstances. You are asked to do the same here.

Shortly after the jurors began their deliberations, they sent me a note stating, "We would like to see the video footage." I had them return to the courtroom to see it once more. Within minutes, after they were sent back to the jury room to continue their deliberations, they reached their guilty verdict.

After the jury was discharged, and while the defendant was wiping away her tears, I wondered why she did not testify. I can understand why most defendants do not want to run the risk of exposing themselves to searing cross-examination by the prosecutor—including disclosure of any past criminal conduct—which could remove any doubts the jurors might have harbored of their guilt. Moreover, since most defendants are guilty, they would be lying under oath, which could result in a higher sentence than otherwise would be the case.

Thus, it would have been foolhardy for Peter Gotti to testify since his checkered criminal past and involvement with the Mafia throughout the years would undoubtedly have surfaced. And perhaps it was wise for Pedro Espada not to testify since it would open the door to having to explain away all of the personal expenditures he wrongfully charged to his health care clinic.

But even though I tell the jurors that a defendant charged with a crime has an absolute constitutional right under the Fifth Amendment not to testify, and that no inferences can be drawn against defendants who exercise that constitutional right, I always wonder whether the jurors—try as they may—can truly resist the temptation to hold that against the defendant.

There are times, therefore, when the smart decision for a defendant would be to take the testimonial risks and swear under oath that he or she is innocent. Thus, although I thought he lied on the witness stand, Anthony Praddy probably beat being convicted for murder because he testified. The jury obviously was influenced by his youthful, plaintive look and his absolute insistence that he did not kill Kevon Simon— although to this day I have my doubts.

I thought that the only way Chevelle Nesbeth could surmount the damning evidence against her and her improbable defense would be to throw herself at the mercy of the jury. With the copious tears that would undoubtedly have flowed, and her whistle-clean background, the jury might have believed that she was duped into allowing the dope to be placed into her suitcase and given her a pass even though it believed that she was guilty. We call this "jury nullification," and I have witnessed it on several occasions, particularly in gun cases where, even though it is a crime to carry a gun without a permit in

New York, jurors are loath to convict, given that reportedly more than 100 million people carry weapons in our country.

The Punishment

As fate would have it, a few weeks before I had to sentence Chevelle Nesbeth, I read Michelle Alexander's book *The New Jim Crow*. Alexander was a former law clerk for the late Supreme Court justice Harry Blackmun—of *Roe v. Wade* fame—and was now a visiting professor of social justice at the Union Theological Seminary. Her book had garnered many awards and had made the bestseller lists of the *New York Times* and the *Washington Post*. In it, Professor Alexander argued that the spate of state and federal statutory collateral consequences facing ex-cons "effectively prevent their reintegration into the mainstream society and economy," amounting "to a form of 'civi[l] death.'" Her particular focus was on the fallout from the "War on Drugs," which she convincingly argued fell disproportionally on young African Americans. She painted a chilling image of this "modern civil death."

> Today a criminal freed from prison has scarcely more rights, and arguably less respect, than a freed slave or a black person living "free" in Mississippi at the height of Jim Crow. Those released from prison on parole can be stopped and searched by the police for any reason . . . and returned to a prison for the most minor of infractions, such as failing to attend a meeting with a parole officer. . . . The "whites only" sign may be gone, but new signs have gone up—notices placed in job applications, rental agreements, loan applications, forms for welfare benefits, school applications, and petitions for licenses, informing the general public that "felons" are not wanted here. A criminal record today authorizes precisely the forms of discrimination we supposedly left behind—discrimination in employment, housing, education, public benefits, and jury service. Those labeled criminals can even be denied the right to vote.

I thought the book was a little over the top and objectively suffered somewhat from Alexander's strident language, but it got me thinking about Chevelle Nesbeth, how she foolishly messed up her life, and what was in store for her after I sentenced her.

I had my law clerks do a little research. They found that the American Bar Association (ABA) had recently established a database of statutes governing the lives of ex-offenders. I was astonished when I learned that there were more than fifty thousand state and more than fifteen hundred federal statutes and regulations that impose penalties, disabilities, or disadvantages on ex-cons. Under federal law alone, a felony conviction could render one ineligible for public housing, section 8 vouchers, Social Security benefits, supplemental nutritional benefits, student loans and legal services corporation representation in public-housing eviction proceedings.

Of the more than a thousand sentences I had rendered during my more than two decades on the bench, I knew that the defendants would naturally have a tough time getting on with their lives. Their lawyers would invariably argue that most employers would be hesitant to hire a convicted felon, and the stigma of being a criminal would obviously make it tough to reenter society. But they never once spoke specifically about the thousands of statutory restrictions that their clients faced after they served their sentence, other than deportation if the defendant was not a citizen. And until I read Alexander's book and checked out the ABA database, I never realized the scope or dimension of these collateral consequences.

My curiosity got the best of me and I wanted to find out what statutory restrictions Nesbeth would be subjected to. So I threw the gauntlet down when I first spoke to the lawyers prior to rendering my sentence, and gave them a little "homework assignment." I wanted them to research and identify the specific statutory collateral consequences Chevelle Nesbeth might face after she served her sentence. And I wanted them to research the law and give me their legal opinion as to whether such consequences should "be part of the 3553(a) mix."

As experienced criminal lawyers, Scotti and David knew what 3553(a) was. Under the sentencing regime, in determining what sentence to impose, judges must consider the factors identified in that section of the criminal code. On the one hand, they must consider "the nature and circumstances of the offense," but on the other hand they must balance and weigh that against "the history and characteristics of the defendant." The "sixty-four-dollar question" I wanted the lawyers to wrestle with was whether I could lawfully add the defendant's statutory collateral consequences to that mix.

I never did that before, nor had any lawyer ever talked to me about it, but I told the government prosecutor and Nesbeth's lawyer that while I did not condone the defendant's criminal behavior, I was "looking at sentencing with some different eyes" that I didn't have before I read Professor Alexander's provocative book and learned about the ABA database.

David told me she had read the book. Scotti had never heard of it. I told him he "would be impressed." I adjourned the sentence and gave the lawyers ample time to complete their homework assignment since I told them "I really am looking forward to a lot of input."

It dawned on me after I left the courtroom that I probably never would have thought about collateral consequences if I had never read Alexander's book, and I wondered if I might have subconsciously been influenced by other books I had recently read. I immensely enjoyed Doris Kearns Goodwin's Team of Rivals, *portraying Lincoln's diverse cabinet and the tensions they wrestled with during the Civil War. And before* Hamilton *hit Broadway, I had read Ron Chernoff's book about the principal author of* The Federalist Papers *and our country's first treasury secretary. I was currently reading* The Devil in the Grove, *Gilbert King's riveting and harrowing account of the literal trials and tribulations of Thurgood Marshall in defending innocent black men facing the noose in Klan country. They were all great works of nonfiction that would be worth reading by anyone interested in our country's history, but I realized that each dealt with the plight of our nation's beleaguered African Americans.*

Could it have been that I was sensitized by the books I had recently read to suddenly take a hard look at the statutory collateral consequences facing convicted African Americans after they reentered society?

⁓

The sentence took place on a sunny day in May 2016. The lawyers had done their homework assignment and submitted letters giving me the benefit of their research and staking out their positions. In addition, I had asked the probation department to update their presentence report, and it had prepared an addendum to its PSR setting forth all the collateral consequences Nesbeth would face.

The probation department calculated her advisory guideline range at thirty-three to forty-one months, but recommended a below guideline sentence because Nesbeth was "a first-time offender, is enrolled in college, and is employed." It also noted that "[s]he has the full support of her mother, with whom she resides, and it appears she has otherwise lived a law-abiding life and is at low risk of recidivism." Nonetheless, the probation department recommended that I put her in jail for twenty-four months.

I had carefully read the PSR, which contained a detailed account of "the offense conduct" and the defendant's "personal and family data." In order to prepare its PSR, the probation officer assigned to her case had met with Nesbeth after she had been convicted and noted in the PSR that, although she chose not to testify at the trial, she then gave him a full post-conviction account of the crime:

> During post-arrest statements, the defendant stated that her boyfriend had asked her if she wanted to make a trip to Jamaica approximately one month prior to the instant trip. She was provided with cash to purchase the airline ticket, and purchased the ticket on December 22, 2014, after the earlier transaction made on her credit card was cancelled due to a problem with the credit card. The defendant had her boyfriend's suitcase to bring to a friend of his. When she arrived in Jamaica, the defendant was retrieved by two friends and they drove her to her family's home in Kingston, Jamaica. At that time, the friends kept the

boyfriend's suitcase. On January 3, 2015, she was brought by the friends to a motel in Montego Bay, where she stayed alone. Three days later, on January 6, 2015, the friends returned and convinced her to bring two new suitcases home, as the one she had was damaged. She was told to bring them to an individual in the United States upon arrival.

The PSR also confirmed Nesbeth's salutary employment history and told me a number of other things about her. "There were no prior trips on her passport," she met the profile of a mere "courier," she had an outstanding $9,000 student loan, she had no history of ever using illegal drugs, and it was not known if she was to receive any money for bringing the suitcases into the country.

I now realized why Nesbeth chose not to testify. Her account of events clearly showed that she was totally complicit, and it was unrealistic to believe that the jury would believe she was an innocent dupe. I thought there was absolutely no excuse for her behavior, and as the sentencing date approached, I believed that some jail time was probably appropriate.

I started the sentencing proceeding by confirming that the PSR correctly calculated the guideline range to be thirty-three to forty-one months. I had carefully read the PSR and all the papers the attorneys had submitted. To its credit, the government did acknowledge that there were indeed statutory collateral consequences for one convicted of a drug felony that were "potentially relevant to the defendant," but opined that "most of the restrictions . . . are not permanent and are lifted after a designated period of time during which the individual engages in no further criminal conduct." It disclosed the following: (1) suspension of eligibility for student assistance programs, including grants, loans, or work assistance programs; (2) denial of federal benefits such as "the issuance of any grant, contract, loan, professional license, or commercial license provided by an agency of or appropriated by funds of the United States"; (3) ineligible for federal-assisted housing; (4) ineligible for Social Security Act/food stamp program benefits; (5) ineligible for passport while on parole or supervised release; (6) revocation or suspension of driver's license.

In addition to that list of federal statutory collateral consequences, Nesbeth's attorney added a few more, but also pointed out that since she was a Connecticut resident, she would also be subject to that state's statutory collateral consequences, including ineligibility for a teaching certificate.

David drew my attention to a recent tentative draft of the Model Penal Code's sentencing provisions created by the American Law Institute, an esteemed organization devoted to recommending model laws designed to improve the quality of our country's laws. As she explained, "the draft suggests that the sentencing commission should as part of its Sentencing Guidelines comprise a list of all collateral consequences both mandatory and discretionary that could be imposed either by state or federal law." She also pointed out that "[m]ore fundamentally, the MPC draft mandates that courts at the time of sentencing ensure that the criminally convicted individual has been apprised of the list of collateral consequences they may face." Finally, David explained that the Model Code "suggested that courts can provide a certificate restoring an individual's rights and demonstrating their rehabilitation after they have shown themselves to be law abiding after a period following sentencing." It "could then be used to obtain lost benefits and opportunities, with the idea being that when a person's sentence has ended so should the additional consequences impacting them."

Once completed, the proposed Model Code could be adopted by Congress and the states, if they chose to do so.

David's conclusion resonated with me:

> At twenty-one years old, Chevelle Nesbeth has her entire life ahead of her. However, the serious consequences that result from her federal drug conviction cannot be overstated. Compacting these consequences with a period of incarceration or

even a lengthy period of supervision would be a severe and an unnecessary punishment.

I thanked each lawyer for the excellent work they had done in accommodating the court's requests, but I wanted to explore the legal issue I had raised before, namely whether I could lawfully consider collateral consequences as a 3553(a) factor in considering a defendant's history and characteristics.

Scotti was somewhat evasive and did not want "to commit the office in any way," but I could understand why since I had done some preliminary research on the subject and surmised that the issue had not been fully explored by the circuit appellate courts; moreover, the Supreme Court had not addressed it. I believed, however, that the Second Circuit, which handles appeals from the New York, Connecticut, and Vermont district courts—and whose decisions I am bound to follow—had in one decision tacitly recognized that collateral consequences could be a 3553(a) consideration.

I decided to take the plunge and hold that I could, and should, take the collateral consequences that Nesbeth would face into consideration as valid 3553(a) factors, and decided I would sentence her to a one-year period of probation.

I also told the lawyers that I had already drafted a written opinion, which I was prepared to now release, fully exploring whether statutory collateral consequences should be a sentencing consideration since the issue appeared to be "something that has been overlooked" by the courts "to a fault." I candidly acknowledged that "I was looking for the right case."

I did, however, require that the defendant be confined to her home for six months "in house arrest," and render one hundred hours of community service so she could serve as a role model "to help dissuade other young people, to even think about violating the law." I also made it perfectly clear to her that her crime was serious and inexcusable and that I did not condone her criminal activities at all.

I then looked directly at Chevelle Nesbeth, standing right in front of me next to her lawyer. The law requires that I give defendants the opportunity to speak to the court before the sentence is officially rendered. I asked her if she wished to speak, hoping that she might acknowledge her culpability, but all she said, in a barely audible voice, was "Thank you for your decision."

Although I had already written the opinion, I wanted to go over it once more before I issued it and it became public. I suspected that it might be controversial because, after all, I was allowing a clearly guilty drug courier to escape prison. As I read it again in the privacy of my office after I left the courtroom, I wondered whether I was really doing the right thing. Was I so committed to writing a leading opinion about an issue that I felt strongly about that I might have been compromising my judicial responsibility to render a proper sentence under the law?

I knew that, in addition to requiring me to consider "the nature and circumstances of the offense and the history and characteristics of the defendant," Section 3553(a) also required me to impose a sentence "(A) to reflect the seriousness of the offense, to promote respect for the law, and to provide just punishment for the offense; (B) to afford adequate deterrence to criminal conduct; and (C) to protect the public from further crimes of the defendant." But I had already bitten the bullet in deciding not to incarcerate Chevelle Nesbeth because of the collateral consequences she was likely to face as a convicted drug felon.

I was troubled, however, that I had made up my mind before I walked into the courtroom that day and that the sentencing proceeding was pretty much a formality. I had always prided myself on keeping an open mind during every sentencing and listening to the lawyers and the defendant before I reached my decision. But I reasoned that Nesbeth was not being prejudiced, and I had carefully considered the government's written submission.

I took one last look at the opinion I had written, saw no reason to change it, took a deep breath, and told my court clerk to file it.

Collateral Consequences 179

The opinion ran forty-two pages. Referencing Alexander's book, I tried to dramatically frame the reason I was writing it in the opening paragraphs:

> Chevelle Nesbeth was convicted by a jury of importation of cocaine and possession of cocaine with intent to distribute. Her advisory guidelines sentencing range was thirty-three to forty-one months. Nonetheless, I rendered a non-incarceratory sentence today in part because of a number of statutory and regulatory collateral consequences she will face as a convicted felon. I have incorporated those consequences in the balancing of the 18 U.S.C. § 3553(a) factors in imposing a one-year probationary sentence.
>
> I am writing this opinion because from my research and experience over two decades as a district judge, sufficient attention has not been paid at sentencing by me and lawyers—both prosecutors and defense counsel—as well as by the probation department in rendering its presentence reports, to the collateral consequences facing a convicted defendant. And I believe that judges should consider such consequences in rendering a lawful sentence.
>
> There is a broad range of collateral consequences that serve no useful function other than to further punish criminal defendants after they have completed their court-imposed sentences. Many—under both federal and state law—attach automatically upon a defendant's conviction.
>
> The effects of these collateral consequences can be devastating. As Professor Michelle Alexander has explained, "myriad laws, rules, and regulations operate to discriminate against ex-offenders and effectively prevent their reintegration into the mainstream society and economy. These restrictions amount to a form of "civi[l] death and send the unequivocal message that 'they' are no longer part of us."
>
> Preparatory to sentencing Ms. Nesbeth, I afforded counsel the opportunity to opine as to whether collateral consequences should indeed be part of the Section 3553(a) mix, and requested

written submissions. The government was essentially noncommittal. Not surprisingly, the office of the federal defender—which represented Ms. Nesbeth—gave a positive response. Commendably, both parties' submissions detailed the collateral consequences she faces.

Because of the significance that I attach to the need of the criminal justice system to embrace collateral consequences as a sentencing issue, I write extensively, addressing in turn: (1) the history of collateral consequences; (2) the depth and breadth of post-conviction statutory and regulatory collateral consequences; (3) the governing caselaw; (4) Ms. Nesbeth's collateral consequences and the balancing of all Section 3553(a) factors; (5) the shaping of the sentence; and (6) the responsibilities of counsel and the probation department.

After exhaustively discussing all these categories, I concluded the opinion by instructing defense counsel that henceforth they have the responsibility prior to sentencing "to timely inform both the court, as well as his client, of the significant collateral consequences facing the defendant as a result of a conviction." I also wrote that the government has responsibilities: "To the extent that collateral consequences are part of the Section 3553(a) mix, prosecutors have an obligation to be candid with the court at sentencing about the applicable collateral consequences and how much weight they should be accorded." And, recognizing that counsel may not always agree, I stated that "[i]n the event counsel in a future case disagree as to the applicability or relevance of certain collateral consequences to a defendant's situation, a hearing may be appropriate to make a factual determination on the issue."

Lastly, I instructed the probation department to "include a collateral-consequences section in all future presentence reports," and urged the legislative branches of our government to act:

> While consideration of the collateral consequences a convicted felon must face should be part of a sentencing judge's calculus in arriving at a just punishment, it does nothing, of course, to mitigate the fact that those consequences will still attach. It is

for Congress and the states' legislatures to determine whether the plethora of postsentence punishments imposed upon felons is truly warranted, and to take a hard look at whether they do the country more harm than good.

I ended the opinion by hoping that "it will be of value to the bench and bar, and to all those who are committed to serving the ends of justice."

I am always concerned of where the line should be drawn in exercising my judicial powers. I try to "keep to the law" and recognize that my function is to apply it and to leave it to the other branches of government to change it. But I also believe that it is my judicial responsibility to call attention to injustices that need to be fixed. When I think about retiring, I think about missing out on the chance that something else may come my way that would give me the opportunity to do that.

As I waited for the response to my decision, I wondered whether I would be chastised for possibly overstepping my judicial bounds or whether it would be viewed as an appropriate exercise of the awesome powers that a single judge has to possibly make some contribution to the administration of justice.

The next day, the *New York Post* did not take kindly to my decision. The headline to its story was "Woman Gets Off Easy for Smuggling $45K of Cocaine," and it followed up with an editorial headlined "Brooklyn Judge Attempts to Rewrite Laws with an Outrageous Wrist-Slap for Drug Felon." But, much to my relief, there was national media reportage praising the decision. The *New York Times* wrote a major article referring to my opinion as "extraordinary," and said that "it is likely to contribute to the national debate about the criminal justice system." It commented that Gabriel J. Chin, a professor at the University of California, Davis School of Law, who had written extensively on the subject, called the opinion "groundbreaking," and that it was "by some distance the most careful and thorough judicial examination" of collateral consequences in sentencing.

Leading national magazines were also praiseworthy. It was a featured piece in the *New Yorker* where the author reported that "federal judges throughout the country have been sending it to one another as a cutting-edge view on an important issue in sentencing." *Slate* led with the headline "In a Remarkable Decision, Federal Judge Lays Out All the Ways Our Justice System Hurts Ex-Cons," and there were a slew of others. I particularly was pleased with the comment in *Vice* that "rather than an aberration by one rogue jurist, some experts see the sentence handed down as a sign of a possible trend where judges look at a broken criminal justice system and take matters into their own hands." And I also liked how it concluded its article:

> If nothing else, the ruling is a reminder that whoever's in the White House next year, and regardless of what federal or local lawmakers decide to do about the ongoing national panic attack that is the war on drugs, it's people—judges and prosecutors—who run the justice system. A fresh injection of humanity into the lifeblood of American law enforcement seems like a welcome adjustment.

But I was perhaps most pleased by what the Heritage Foundation had written:

> Collateral consequences of criminal conviction are civil disabilities imposed by local, state, and federal lawmakers and sometimes by administrative bodies. They are distinct from the direct consequences, such as a criminal record, fines, probation, and prison, and are often premised on the need to protect public safety once an offender is released. While some are certainly justifiable, collateral consequences that are applied indiscriminately with a tenuous relationship between the restriction imposed and the offense committed, can make it more difficult for someone with a criminal record to reintegrate into society, thereby

increasing the likelihood that an ex-offender will return to a life of crime and recidivate. Legislators should reassess existing collateral consequences to ensure that, rather than merely being imposed as an additional punishment, they truly make sense from a public safety standpoint. Legislators should also reinvigorate or create, if necessary, some procedural mechanisms for ex-offenders to receive relief from unduly onerous collateral consequences in deserving cases.

The Heritage Foundation is a conservative public policy think tank that took a leading role in the conservative movement during the presidency of Ronald Reagan, whose policies were taken from Heritage's policy study, Mandate for Leadership.

After I read what had been written about my opinion, I realized that it had crossed ideological lines. I could not have been more pleased. I just try to reach what I believe to be the right result. I am often amused that sometimes my decisions have been viewed as the handiwork of "one of those liberal judges," and on other occasions they are looked upon favorably "by the conservatives." The truth is that I don't see myself as either a liberal or conservative judge; I see myself as just a judge, and I have no use for branding judges by labels. I often think about the times I have sat as a designated circuit court judge for the Ninth Circuit, which has somewhat of an undeserved reputation for being politically polarized, and am always impressed with how the judges, regardless of their political persuasions, invariably just try to "get it right." I think Chief Justice Roberts was correct when he recently commented: "We do not have Obama judges or Trump judges, Bush judges or Clinton judges. What we have is an extraordinary group of dedicated judges doing their level best to do equal right to those appearing before them. That independent judiciary is something we should all be thankful for."

To be sure, there are those controversial 5–4 decisions by the high court dealing with a handful of critical issues dividing the country where ideology has made a difference, but the independence of the judiciary remains paramount.

~

As I was finishing this final chapter of the book, I was curious to learn how Chevelle Nesbeth was doing, since it had now been more than two years since I had sentenced her. I reached out to her lawyer, Ms. David, who told me that Nesbeth had completed her probation without incident and was expecting to graduate from college soon. However, since her dreams of becoming a teacher and, perhaps a principal, were no longer realistic, she had shifted her major studies to psychology because she felt that she could effectively counsel people who had also "been through the system." But although some states had adopted the American Law Institute's Model Code on Collateral Consequences, Connecticut had not, and she had to adjust to living with both the stigma of being an ex-con as well as with all the adverse statutory collateral consequences that were still attached to her.

Moreover, she could never have her criminal conviction expunged. Although my former Brooklyn district court judicial colleague John Gleeson had written a forward-looking decision, before he returned to private practice, expunging a thirteen-year-old fraud conviction that was preventing a law-abiding ex-offender from getting employment, the circuit court on appeal reversed his holding, ruling that there was no present basis under federal law to permit expungement.

Nevertheless, there appears to be a growing national consensus that with more than two million people presently incarcerated in our country, half of which are drug related, intelligent, rational sentencing reform is long overdue. Happily, as I am now writing this part of the book, Congress is in the throes of passing a major sentencing reform bill.

Recent statistics estimate that seventy million people in the United States have a serious misdemeanor or felony arrest or conviction record that could impact their ability to find a job. Moreover, each year about 630,000 people on average are released from state and federal prisons across the country after completing their sentence, and about five million are on parole or probation under community supervision. They each have to find a way to make ends meet while saddled with their ubiquitous collateral consequences.

I am often asked, as are most judges, which is the most important case you have ever handled. I always say it was Nesbeth.

Coda

Many times I have been asked whether I have ever sentenced an innocent person to jail. I have also asked that question to many of my judicial colleagues. Not surprisingly, not one, including myself, has ever said that she or he did. But how do we really know for sure? Guilt or innocence is determined by jurors, not robots, and the human being is hardly an infallible animal.

What we do know is that while I and my judicial colleagues on my court believe that we never have jailed an innocent person, thousands of innocent people have been convicted; conversely, many who should be in jail are walking the streets as free people. I recently read that more than thirty thousand innocent people are in jail, although I don't know the basis for that statistic. But we know that, principally with the advent of DNA evidence, more than 160 people on death row have been exonerated, and we suspect that some innocent people may have been executed.

While this book has dealt with the sentencing of those who either pleaded guilty or were found guilty by a jury, I could not end it without talking about those who have been sentenced after they had been wrongfully convicted—as it later turned out—by overzealous and ethically challenged prosecutors. It is a huge scandal that has recently come dramatically to life in my district, and has triggered debate as to whether such prosecutors should be held accountable for their egregious behavior.

My involvement with the issue all started with the *Collins* case. Jabbar Collins had been in jail for sixteen years for a crime he did not commit until he was freed a few years ago by my colleague Chief Judge Irizzary after it was discovered that his prosecutor from the Brooklyn DA's office failed to turn over exculpatory evidence to Collins's trial lawyer: all the principal witnesses at the trial had recanted but the prosecutor chose not to tell anyone.

After he was freed, Collins brought a civil lawsuit against the prosecutor, the Brooklyn DA, and the city of New York seeking compensation for the many years he had been behind bars. I had to dismiss the case against the prosecutor and the DA because under the law they were entitled to absolute immunity. But I did not dismiss the city of New York because, under what is known as *Monell* liability, it could be held liable for their misdeeds. Soon after, Collins settled his lawsuit with the city for $10 million.

But the settlement was only the tip of the iceberg. Ultimately, more than twenty-five other wrongful convictions because of prosecutorial misconduct by Brooklyn prosecutors were unearthed, mostly against poor, young African Americans who had, like Collins, spent years in jail. They have led to an estimated $400 million in settlements from taxpayer monies. And other wrongful convictions have recently been overturned elsewhere throughout New York State and in other parts of the country.

Shockingly, no action has been taken against the Brooklyn prosecutors and they remain unscathed. However, this all led to the legislation creating the state's Prosecutorial Misconduct Commission.

I had been asked by proponents of the legislation whether I, as the author of the Collins opinion, would be willing to pen an editorial urging passage of the bill. It put me in the position of having to decide whether to hide behind my judicial robes or to speak out against perpetuating what I believed was a miscarriage of justice that sorely needed to be publicly addressed. I chose the latter, but not without reflecting on whether a judge should take an active role in publicly addressing issues about which he has acquired unique knowledge and insight during the course of his judicial calling.

I end the book, therefore, with the way I began, raising the controversial question of whether a judge should speak out or remain silent on matters of importance to the public. I recognize that my choice may not be shared by many of my colleagues, but it is a matter of fair debate.

My hope is that by raising awareness of some of the profound issues facing a sentencing judge that I have identified in this book, I will have constructively opened the door to more judicial openness and less secrecy.

Acknowledgments

This book would not have happened if not for John Palmer, the American Bar Association's Executive Editor. I had sent John the first few chapters and he encouraged me to finish it. While he did not think that it fell into any discernible category of books traditionally published by the ABA, he nonetheless thought it merited publication because he believed that both the legal community and the general public would find value in the book and would enjoy reading it. John got the necessary approval from the ABA committee that decides which proposed books are worthy of publication, and also gave me valuable editorial suggestions.

A special thanks goes to Thomson-Reuters, which published my first book, *Disrobed: An Inside Look at the Life and Work of a Federal Trial Judge,* for its permission to borrow extensively from the chapter on Racketeering, recounting the trial of Peter Gotti and his fellow Gambino-family co-defendants. I am particularly grateful to TR's Darcie Bahr, who edited *Disrobed,* and to Jeff McCoy, TR's Director of Communications, for their continued post-*Disrobed* support of my literary efforts to share with the public my thoughts and experiences as a federal district judge throughout my judicial career.

And then there were my judicial colleagues and friends who gave me valuable feedback. In no necessary order, I thank Judges Raymond Dearie and Brian Cogan, Steve Edwards, Ron Holzer, Frank Velie, John Horan, Steve Zissou, Gary Villanueva, and Wendy Bacher.

Family members were also supportive. First, of course, was my wife Betsy, a constant fan and supporter of all my literary efforts. And thanks also go to my brother Leonard and sister-in-law Naomi, as well as to my daughters, Tina and Debbie.

And last, I am most grateful to my law clerks, Ty Cone, Adena Wayne, and Leonid Grinberg, for their substantive and editorial help during their free time.

About the Author

Frederic Block was appointed United States District Judge for the Eastern District of New York on September 29, 1994. He received a bachelor's degree from Indiana University in 1956 and an LLB degree from Cornell Law School in 1959.

Judge Block has been described by Alan Ellis, a nationally recognized authority on sentencing and a past president of the National Association of Criminal Defense Lawyers, as a "legendary sentencing judge." Judge Block continues to maintain a full caseload, as a senior judge, after twenty-four years on the bench. He has presided over many high-profile cases, including the trials of former Bear Stearns hedge fund managers Ralph Cioffi and Matthew Tannin, Kenneth "Supreme" McGriff, Peter Gotti, Lemrick Nelson, and nightclub magnate Peter Gatien. Judge Block also regularly sits by designation on the Ninth Circuit Court of Appeals, where he has authored over a dozen opinions.

Judge Block recently authored the "reality-fiction" novel *Race to Judgment*, after having written his highly-acclaimed memoir *Disrobed, An Inside Look at the Life and Work of a Federal Trial Judge*. He also coauthored the 1985 off-Broadway musical *Professionally Speaking* (book, music, and lyrics), and has published many articles on a variety of legal topics.